gales

Kori kelly

To: kummy
from: mom

I love
scince . . .

one million things

SCIENCE

**LONDON, NEW YORK,
MELBOURNE, MUNICH, AND DELHI**

For Tall Tree Ltd:
Editors Rob Colson, Jon Richards, and Jennifer Sanderson
Designers Malcolm Parchment and Ed Simkins

For DK Publishing:
Senior editor Victoria Heyworth-Dunne
Senior designer Smiljka Surla

Managing editor Linda Esposito
Managing art editor Jim Green

Creative retouching Steve Willis
Picture research Louise Thomas

Category publisher Laura Buller

DK picture researcher Emma Shepherd
Production editor Marc Staples
Senior production controller Angela Graef

Jacket design Hazel Martin
Jacket editor Matilda Gollon
Design development manager Sophia M. Tampakopoulos Turner
Development team Yumiko Tahata

First published in the United States in 2011 by
DK Publishing
375 Hudson Street
New York, New York 10014

10 9 8 7 6 5 4 3 2 1
001—179074—June/11

DK books are available at special discounts when purchased in bulk for
sales promotions, premiums, fund-raising, or educational use. For details, contact:
DK Publishing Special Markets, 375 Hudson Street, New York, New York 10014 or SpecialSales@dk.com.

A catalog record for this book is available
from the Library of Congress.

ISBN: 978-0-7566-8260-6

Printed and bound by Leo, China

**Discover more at
www.dk.com**

one million things

SCIENCE

Written by:
Clive Gifford
Consultant:
Lisa Burke

1

The Living World   6
Life on Earth   8
Plant structure   10
Plant reproduction   12
Evolution and extinction   14
Insects and arachnids   16
Reptiles and amphibians   18
Birds   20
Underwater life   22
Mammals   24
Ecosystems   26
Human body   28
Skeleton and muscles   30
Blood and breathing   32
The digestive system   34
Brain and senses   36
Body repair   38
Genetics   40

2

Earth   42
Earth's origins   44
Plates and faults   46
Earthquakes and volcanoes   48
Rocks and soil   50
Weathering and erosion   52
Fossils and strata   54
Water   56
Weather   58
Natural resources   60
Human impact   62

3

Matter and materials   64
Building blocks   66
The periodic table   68
States of matter   70
Properties of matter   72
Chemical reactions   74
Mixtures and compounds   76
Acids, bases, and salts   78
Materials science   80

4

Energy and forces 82
Energy 84
Forces 86
Motion 88
Simple machines 90
Electromagnetic spectrum 92
Sound 94
Heat 96
Light 98
Electricity 100
Magnetism 102
Using electricity 104

5

Space 106
The Universe 108
Galaxies and stars 110
Star life and death 112
The Solar System 114
Sun and Moon 116
Asteroids, meteorites, and comets 118
Seeing into space 120
Space exploration 122

Glossary 124
Index 126
Acknowledgments 128

Contents

FULL OF LIFE
A coral reef is packed with marine life. Different species of fish, crustaceans, marine plants, and mammals, as well as billions of microscopic plankton, make the waters around a coral reef their home.

The Living World

LIFE ON EARTH

Life exists in rich abundance on Earth. A species is a group of living organisms, such as humans, golden eagles, and blue whales, which share common characteristics and can breed with each other. Scientists have identified almost two million different species, although there may be many more. These are divided up into five kingdoms—plants, animals, fungi, bacteria, and single-celled organisms known as protists. All share some basic characteristics of life that enable them to survive.

▼ MOVEMENT

Living things are capable of moving part or all of their bodies. Plants may be rooted in one place, but they can grow in different directions and their flowers can open and close. This cougar (also known as a puma or mountain lion) is the largest predatory animal in the United States. It can run at speeds of more than 30 mph (50 km/h) in short sprints.

▲ FOOD ENERGY

All living things require food, which they digest for energy to fuel their movement, to maintain and repair their bodies, and for growth. Animals that eat other creatures are called carnivores, such as this osprey catching a fish. Animals that eat only plants are called herbivores, while those that eat both plants and animals are called omnivores. Plants make food through the process of photosynthesis, while fungi feed on decaying plant and animal matter.

An eagle's talons are sharp and can grip prey securely

▼ RESPIRATION

Respiration is the release of energy from food substances in all living cells. It is a chemical reaction and it can be either aerobic (with oxygen) or anaerobic (without oxygen). Animals, such as this polar bear, respire aerobically, taking in oxygen from the surrounding air or, in the case of fish, from water. The oxygen is exchanged in a land animal's lungs, a fish's gills, or an insect's tracheas with carbon dioxide, which respiration creates as a waste product.

Powerful hind leg muscles enable cougars to leap up to 30 ft (9 m)

Cell division creates new cells essential for reproduction and growth

The cell divides into two with identical nuclei in the center of each new cell

▲ REPRODUCTION

All living things reproduce to create offspring—new individuals of the species. Asexual reproduction is found in bacteria, some plants, and other creatures. It involves just one parent that may divide in two or features a part that breaks off to form an identical offspring. Sexual reproduction involves male and female parents who create a new offspring with a mixture of traits from the two parents.

▼ GROWTH

All plants and animals are capable of growth. They use food to create new cells and to increase their size. Plants grow from seedlings into mature specimens, while animals grow from young to adults. The Pacific giant kelp is one of the fastest growing organisms on Earth. It is capable of growing by as much as 20 in (50 cm) per day.

▶ RESPONSIVENESS

All living things have an awareness of their surroundings and are able to respond to their environment. An animal may respond to sound, heat, or light with specially adapted nerve cells sending signals from one part of the body to another. Plants are sensitive to gravity with stems growing upward and roots growing downward. They also respond to light by bending toward light sources. This is known as phototropism.

PLANT STRUCTURE

There are more than 300,000 species of plants, ranging in size from the minute species of *Wolffia* (members of the duckweed family) to giant sequoia trees, the largest of which stand more than 330 ft (100 m) high. Botanists divide plants into those that produce flowers and those that are nonflowering. Along with some bacteria, plants are the only living things that manufacture their own food through photosynthesis.

▶ TRANSPORTATION

Most plants are vascular, containing special cells that transport vital substances. This cross section through a sunflower stem shows the xylem cells that transport water and some dissolved mineral nutrients from the roots up through the plant. Outside the xylem cells are phloem cells, which carry sugars created during photosynthesis around the plant.

Phloem cells   Xylem cells

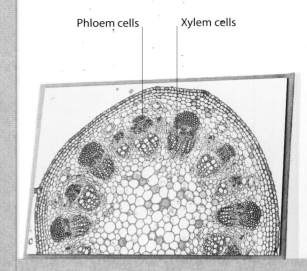

▶ PLANT STRUCTURE

Plants are divided into vascular plants, which contain tissues that transport water, nutrients, and food around the plant (see above), and nonvascular plants, such as mosses and liverworts. A seedling of a young hazel tree already shows the parts that vascular plants share. Its roots bind it into the soil, while its stem supports its branches and leaves. Young stems rely on the pressure of water to stay upright, but gradually stiffen as the plant grows.

Leaves release water and manufacture food

Stem of plant supports the branches and leaves

Growth of new branch

Root network branches out in the soil

Seed from which the shoot has grown up and the root has grown down

Primary root grows downward

▼ LEAVES

Leaves are mostly flat structures connected to a stem by a stalk, called the petiole. A network of veins runs through the leaf, carrying water and nutrients to the leaf and glucose from it to other parts of the plant. Leaves are made up of different layers of cells. The palisade layer has chloroplasts, which contain chlorophyll, a chemical that gives plants their green color. It is in the chloroplasts that photosynthesis occurs.

Tough, waterproof outer layer called the cuticle

Epidermis layer covers outer part of leaf

Palisade layer forms upper part of mesophyll

Spongy layer forms lower part of mesophyll

10

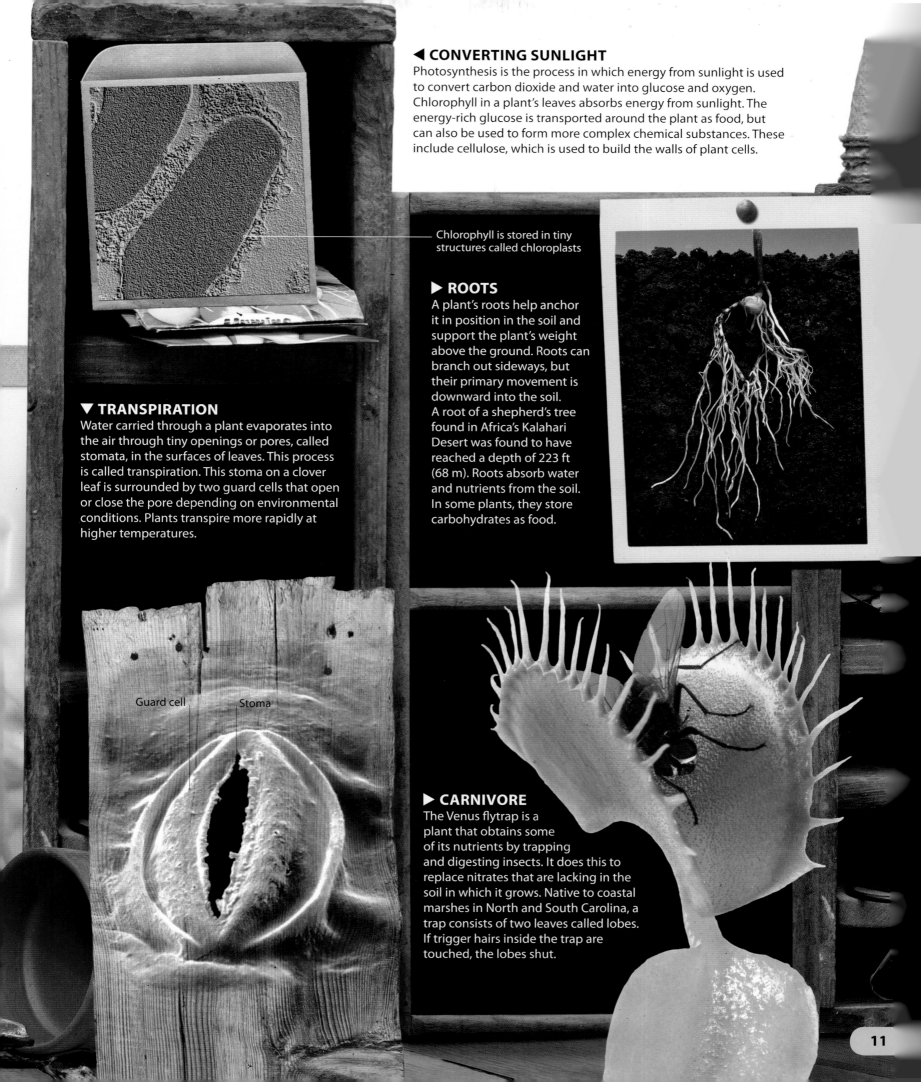

◄ CONVERTING SUNLIGHT

Photosynthesis is the process in which energy from sunlight is used to convert carbon dioxide and water into glucose and oxygen. Chlorophyll in a plant's leaves absorbs energy from sunlight. The energy-rich glucose is transported around the plant as food, but can also be used to form more complex chemical substances. These include cellulose, which is used to build the walls of plant cells.

Chlorophyll is stored in tiny structures called chloroplasts

▶ ROOTS

A plant's roots help anchor it in position in the soil and support the plant's weight above the ground. Roots can branch out sideways, but their primary movement is downward into the soil. A root of a shepherd's tree found in Africa's Kalahari Desert was found to have reached a depth of 223 ft (68 m). Roots absorb water and nutrients from the soil. In some plants, they store carbohydrates as food.

▼ TRANSPIRATION

Water carried through a plant evaporates into the air through tiny openings or pores, called stomata, in the surfaces of leaves. This process is called transpiration. This stoma on a clover leaf is surrounded by two guard cells that open or close the pore depending on environmental conditions. Plants transpire more rapidly at higher temperatures.

Guard cell   Stoma

▶ CARNIVORE

The Venus flytrap is a plant that obtains some of its nutrients by trapping and digesting insects. It does this to replace nitrates that are lacking in the soil in which it grows. Native to coastal marshes in North and South Carolina, a trap consists of two leaves called lobes. If trigger hairs inside the trap are touched, the lobes shut.

11

PLANT REPRODUCTION

Plants need to reproduce for their species to survive. New plants replace those that die, increase the population numbers, and distribute a plant species to new locations. Flowering plants produce seeds that, if the temperature and conditions are suitable, will begin growing into new plants—a process called germination. Seeds are often dispersed to avoid competing for the same light, water, and soil nutrients as their parent plant.

❶ FLOWERS

There are more than 250,000 different species of flowering plants. Flowers contain both male and female sex organs. Some plants, such as oak trees, produce separate male and female flowers. The female sex cells, or ovaries, lie at the base of a stalk called a pistil. At the top of the pistil lies a sticky or feathery structure called the stigma. The male sex cells, called pollen, are located on other stalks called stamens.

❷ POLLINATION

For sexual reproduction to occur, male sex cells have to reach female sex cells. This process is called pollination. Some plants' flowers can self-pollinate, but most rely on cross-pollination, with pollen traveling from one plant to another. Wind transports pollen from some types of plants. Others rely on creatures, such as bees, carrying pollen from one flower to another.

❸ SEEDS AND FRUITS

When pollination is successful, seeds form inside fruits. The seeds may be surrounded by a hard casing or protected by a fleshy covering. The fruit helps the seed disperse from the parent plant by rolling away when dropped or by being eaten by creatures and deposited in their droppings. Seeds contain a food store to sustain life until they germinate into plants and can produce food through photosynthesis.

❶ Stigma

Pistil

Stamen   Ovary

Leaf edge

Buds

❷

❸

❹

❹ VEGETATIVE REPRODUCTION

Vegetative reproduction does not involve flowers, pollination, and seeds. Instead, a new plant grows out from the stem or leaf of a parent plant. The Mexican hat plant, native to Madagascar, produces seeds from its flowers. It can also reproduce vegetatively by creating new plants from small buds that form along the edges of its leaves before dropping off.

❺ NONFLOWERING PLANTS

Plants without flowers do not produce seeds. Most produce spores that are surrounded by a protective casing. Ferns grow large quantities of spores in capsules called sporangia, usually under their leaves. When these capsules open, the spores are blown over long distances.

❻ STUCK ON YOU

Some plant seeds have sticky hairs or hooks that attach to the bodies of animals or the clothing of humans to carry them away. Viewed under a microscope, the cocklebur's seeds have a series of tiny hooks known as burrs. These easily tangle in the fur or hair of an animal's coat, and the animal then transports the seed to a new location.

❼ WIND DISPERSAL

A dandelion head contains many individual seeds. Each is connected by a long filament to a parachute that catches a breeze easily, causing the seed to be carried away from the plant. Other plants, such as the sycamore tree, enclose seeds in winglike outer husks, which drift away on air currents.

❽ SQUIRTING PODS

Squirting cucumbers (pictured) are members of the gourd family of plants. They group their seeds together surrounded by an outer shell, called a pod. When it is ripe, the seed pod of the squirting cucumber releases a jet of liquid containing the plant's seeds. This ensures that the seeds are spread far enough away from the parent plant to encourage growth.

❾ WATER DISPERSAL

Plants that grow next to rivers, streams, and along coasts often rely on water to disperse their seeds. Coconuts are palm-tree seeds that can survive in seawater for several months. The seed remains dormant until it encounters freshwater and begins to grow.

Sporangia

Spores

Seed pod

EVOLUTION AND EXTINCTION

Over long periods of time, living things have gradually altered as the conditions around them change. A species' strongest traits are passed from one generation to the next. This process of gradual change is called evolution. Some species fail to evolve, becoming extinct. Although millions of species are now extinct, fossil records of their previous existence remain.

▶ BIRD EVOLUTION

Fossil evidence of creatures that are now extinct is studied and used to show the paths that evolution has taken as species have evolved. The discovery of *Archaeopteryx*, a creature that lived about 150 million years ago, shows how birds evolved from lizards. Like lizards of the time, *Archaeopteryx* had teeth, a strong jaw, and bony-fingered claws. It also had wings and feathers.

▶ INTERESTING ADAPTATIONS

Creatures have evolved unusual adaptations to survive and prosper in their environment. The aye-aye lives in the forests of Madagascar. Its long middle finger can grow up to 6 in (15 cm) long. It is used for tapping trees to listen for hollows that contain insects and larvae, the creature's main source of food.

◀ NATURAL SELECTION

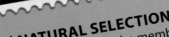

The principle that the members of a species that adapt best to an environment survive, reproduce, and pass on their adaptations to the next generation is called natural selection. Over many generations, these tiny alterations can lead to major changes. Musk oxen, for example, have developed thick outer coats of long hairs over a second layer of wool-like fibers to survive the freezing temperatures of the Arctic.

▶ VESTIGIAL STRUCTURES

Living in the waters of dark underground caves, the blind cave fish cannot see, yet its head still contains eyes. This is an example of a vestigial structure: a feature that once worked, but is no longer of use. Other examples are partly developed rear legs in some whales and the remains of a tail at the base of the human spine, called the coccyx.

MASS EXTINCTION ▲

Extinction is the dying out of an entire species. Extinctions have occurred regularly throughout Earth's history. At certain times, major climatic changes, catastrophic events such as large meteorite impacts, or massive volcanic activity on Earth have caused the extinction of large numbers of species. Around 65 million years ago, the Cretaceous-Tertiary extinction event saw about three-quarters of all species, including the dinosaurs, die out.

▶ RECENT EXTINCTIONS

Hunting, habitat destruction, pollution, and introducing competing species are four major ways in which humans have helped bring about or speed up extinctions. The dodo was a large, flightless bird from Mauritius that became extinct around 1680. Its extinction was caused by hunting and by dogs introduced to the island by traders.

Siberian tiger

Mountain gorilla

◀ ENDANGERED

Thousands of species are at risk of extinction despite the efforts of conservation groups. These include the Siberian tiger and the mountain gorilla. Fewer than 700 of both creatures are believed to still live in the wild. The Iberian lynx is also endangered due to habitat destruction and deaths caused by rabbit traps.

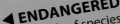
Iberian lynx

INSECTS AND ARACHNIDS

There are more species of insects than any other creature. Within this incredible diversity, nearly all insects share common features. All are invertebrates (creatures without backbones). They have a hard outer covering, called an exoskeleton, which supports their bodies and is segmented into three parts: the head, thorax, and abdomen. Insects have six jointed legs and most insects have wings, although some, such as the silverfish, do not. Arachnids have an abdomen, head, thorax, and eight legs.

▼ BUTTERFLIES AND MOTHS

Butterflies, such as this white admiral, are usually active during the day. They have large, flat wings and long tubular mouthparts which they use to feed on nectar. Moths are similar to butterflies, but tend to be most active at night and rest with their wings open rather than closed. There are more than 150,000 species of butterflies and moths.

▲ FLIES

True flies include houseflies, gnats, mosquitoes, and crane flies. They are insects that have just one pair of wings with their second, rear pair reduced to knoblike structures called halteres. The halteres help them balance during flight. Flies are among the fastest and most maneuverable insects in flight. They have compound eyes that contain many lenses, which provide extremely accurate 3-D vision.

Compound eye

Wings

▲ METAMORPHOSIS

Many insects lay eggs that go through dramatic stages of development, known as metamorphosis, before becoming adults. Butterflies and bees are among those insects that hatch from eggs as larvae. Once reaching full size, the larvae enter a pupating stage during which their bodies are broken down and then reassembled to emerge as adults.

After mating, a female butterfly will lay eggs on a leaf

After about 24 hours, an adult butterfly emerges from the chrysalis

A citrus swallowtail larva is a butterfly that caterpillar feeds on leaves

The caterpillar spins a cocoon of thread around itself called a chrysalis

▼ ORTHOPTERA

Grasshoppers, crickets, katydids, and locusts are all *orthoptera* insects. From eggs, they undergo incomplete metamorphosis as their larvae are much like adults, only they lack an adult's two pairs of wings. Adult *orthoptera* can make a distinctive sound by rubbing body parts together.

Pincers used to hold prey

Grasshoppers communicate by rubbing their hind legs against their wings

▶ SCORPIONS

Scorpions are a type of arachnid. Their bodies feature two large pincers and, at the rear, a segmented tail. Their tails have a stinger supplied with venom by two sacs. Scorpions mostly live in warm and dry tropical regions and are nocturnal, hunting at night for insects and spiders as their prey.

Stinger used to paralyze or kill prey

▼ SPIDERS

Like scorpions, spiders are arachnids. They have eight legs, each with seven jointed parts and more than 30 muscles. Their bodies are divided into an abdomen, and a head and thorax fused together, which contains the spider's brain and stomach. Spiders are carnivorous and most kill their prey with venom.

BEES AND WASPS ▲

Bees and wasps are related to ants. Bees pollinate large numbers of flowering plants as they feed on nectar. Wasps feed their young on insects. Only female bees and wasps have powerful stingers at the tips of their abdomens. Many species of wasps and most bees are social and live in large nests or hives.

▼ ANTS

Ants form specialized colonies containing just one or a handful of queens—the only females capable of reproduction. Leafcutter-ant colonies can contain eight million members. Leafcutter ants have powerful vibrating jaws that can slice rapidly through leaves. They can carry leaf material weighing 20 times their body weight.

▶ HEMIPTERA

The group of insects known as true bugs, or *hemiptera*, includes aphids, cicadas, stink bugs, and pond skaters (right). They have beak-shaped mouthparts that pierce then suck up liquid food, such as the sap from plants. Some, like the pond skater, are carnivorous and feed on other insects.

▼ BEETLES

More than 350,000 species of beetles have been identified, more than any other type of insect. A beetle's front wings, called elytra, are hardened and can be closed over the top of the abdomen, protecting the rear pair of wings. The biggest species of beetle is the South American longhorn, which can grow up to 6 in (16 cm) in length.

17

REPTILES AND AMPHIBIANS

Reptiles are land-dwelling creatures with tough skins covered with scales. All reptiles are vertebrates (they have backbones) and most have four legs, although snakes and worm lizards do not. For about 200 million years, giant reptiles called dinosaurs were the world's largest creatures. Amphibians were the first vertebrates to move from water to land.

Adult female Nile crocodiles carry their young to a nursery area in the water

▶ COLD-BLOODED

Reptiles and amphibians are ectothermic, or cold-blooded. They are unable to generate their own body heat and thus cannot regulate their own body temperature. Instead, they bask in the sun to warm up and dip their bodies in water to cool down. Some collared and frilly lizards run on their hind legs to produce a cooling breeze around themselves.

A common lizard basks in the sun to warm its body up. Its ideal internal temperature is around 86°F (30°C).

▶ REPTILE LIFE CYCLE

A small number of reptiles, including the slow worm and the adder snake, give birth to live young. However, most reptiles lay hard- or leathery-shelled eggs that hatch into live young. The Nile crocodile digs a nest in a river bank before laying up to 80 eggs, which are then covered with sand. The female will guard the nest before the eggs begin to hatch.

Baby Nile crocodiles measure around 12 in (30 cm) long when they hatch

Frog eggs surrounded by jelly

▼ AMPHIBIAN SKINS

Instead of a covering of hair, fur, or scales, an amphibian's skin contains a network of tiny blood capillaries. These enable an amphibian to take in water and oxygen through its skin. For this to work efficiently, the skin needs to be kept moist. Most amphibians secrete a slimy layer of mucus, which keeps the skin from drying. In some amphibians this layer is poisonous to deter potential predators.

Geckos have tiny ridges on the skin beneath their feet, which help them grip sheer walls

Couch's spadefoot toad

▶ REPTILE SKINS

Reptiles have dry skin made of a horny substance called keratin. The upper bodies of turtles and tortoises are covered in hard shells, which protect the body parts underneath. Snakes shed their skin as they grow.

Red-eared slider turtle

▶ AMPHIBIAN LIFE CYCLE

Adult frog

Most amphibians lay their eggs in water. Some species of frogs and toads lay thousands of eggs and abandon them. Others lay fewer eggs but guard them. Amphibian eggs are soft and many species' eggs are surrounded by a jellylike substance to keep them from drying out. A frog's eggs hatch to form tadpoles that develop gills on the outside of the body, and a tail. Tadpoles undergo a major change in body shape as they develop into an infant frog.

Infant frog with tail

Tadpoles

▶ ESTIVATION

Some reptiles and amphibians, such as this cane toad from Australia, can enter a period of inactivity when water is scarce. This is called estivation and is a survival mechanism. Estivating creatures head underground where it is cooler and where some moisture may be found. They lower their heart rate and conserve water in their bodies.

BIRDS

There are more than 9,600 species of birds distributed over every continent. They are the only vertebrates with feathers, and all females lay eggs. Most birds are capable of flight, and their front limbs have evolved into wings covered in feathers. These enable some birds to swoop and dive at high speeds or to soar over long distances for hours at a time.

Lower mandible

Cervical vertebrae

Hollow wing bones

Large keel

Pygostyle supports tail feathers

Ankle joint

Barbs branch off of central shaft

Central shaft

Barb Barbule

◀ SKELETON

Most birds are very light for their size—for example, Australia's wedge-tailed eagle has a wingspan of up to 8 ft (2.5 m), but may weigh only 10 lb (4.5 kg). Part of the secret is in their bones, a number of which are hollow and may be reinforced with internal struts. A bird's skeleton has to be light, but strong enough to fly.

▼ FEATHERS

A bird can have between 800 and 20,000 feathers, which grow and are replaced throughout its life. Feathers consist of a central spine, side branches called barbs, and many smaller branches from the barbs, called barbules. Feathers enable flight, help insulate against water and heat loss, and for some birds act as camouflage or are used to attract a mate.

◀ FLYING MUSCLES

A male great bustard can weigh up to 42 lb (19 kg), making it the heaviest flying bird in the world. Birds rely on powerful breast muscles attached to a developed part of the sternum (breastbone), called the keel. These muscles must generate enough power to become airborne. The downstroke of each wing beat pushes the air down and the bird up and forward.

A toucan's giant bill can grow to one-third of the bird's length.

◀ FLIGHT AGILITY

Many birds exhibit extraordinary flying agility or speed—for example, a diving peregrine falcon can reach 200 mph (320 km/h). Kestrels can hover in midair, seeking out prey on the ground below. A hummingbird can also hover, allowing it to remain in front of a flower as it feeds on plant nectar. Its wings can beat up and down 90 times every second.

▶ FLIGHTLESS BIRDS

Over thousands of years, some bird species have lost their ability to fly. These include seabirds, such as penguins, whose wings are used like flippers to swim. Flightless birds range in size from the 7 in (17 cm) long Inaccessible Island rail to the ostrich, the largest living bird. Male ostriches can be 8 ft (2.5 m) tall and can run at speeds of 43 mph (70 km/h).

Kingfisher's daggerlike beak catches fish and other prey

▲ BEAKS

All birds have some form of bill or beak. Birds use their beaks to preen their feathers, build nests, and feed their young. Beaks show great variety and adaptation for a bird's habitat—for example curlews, sandpipers, and other wading birds, have long, thin beaks for probing sand and mudflats for food. Eagles and other birds of prey have hooked beaks for tearing meat.

Clutch of eggs

Nest of twigs and other plant matter

▲ FUEL

Birds eat food sources that are rich in protein and energy. Kingfishers are one of many species that plunge into water to capture fish, insects, or small amphibians. Other species, such as parrots, eat fruits and nuts. Since they do not have teeth, birds use a part of their stomach called the gizzard to crush and grind down seeds and bony parts.

▲ EGGS AND NESTING

All birds lay eggs, which are kept warm by being either buried, or incubated by the parents sitting on them. Nests offer protection from predators and can be as simple as a shallow hollow in the ground or a mixture of mud and plant matter. Cuckoos are an example of parasitic breeders who lay their eggs in other birds' nests.

UNDERWATER LIFE

Earth's rivers, lakes, seas, and oceans teem with life. More than two-thirds of the planet's surface is covered in water. In deep oceans, most marine life exists in the top 330 ft (100 m) or so, since this is where light and vast quantities of microscopic organisms, called plankton, are most abundant. Plankton is crucial since it forms the basis of marine-life diets. All underwater life either feeds directly on plankton or preys on creatures that do.

▼ CARTILAGINOUS FISH

Skates, rays, and sharks, such as this great white, are all cartilaginous fish. They lack a true backbone, but have a structure made of gristly cartilage. They also lack swim bladders and must maintain their depth by swimming. Most species of sharks are predators. Rays are flattened fish that live on the seabed where they hunt smaller fish.

Sea lion

▲ BONY FISH

Every species of bony fish has a skeleton of bones with a flexible spine, or backbone, running the length of the body. An organ called the swim bladder enables a constant buoyancy, regardless of the changing water pressure. This ocean sunfish is the heaviest bony fish—some weigh as much as 4,400 lb (2,000 kg).

▶ MARINE MAMMALS

Some mammals (see pages 24–25) spend most or all of their lives in water. These include many species of whales, porpoises, and dolphins; and plant-eating dugongs and manatees. All of these creatures must surface to breathe. Other marine mammals, such as this sea lion, along with walruses and seals, are skilled swimmers but must return to land to breed and reproduce.

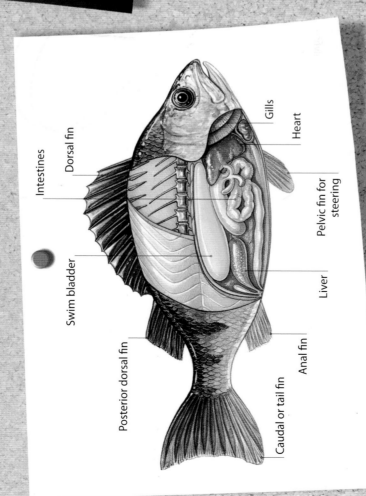

Dorsal fin

Intestines

Gills

Heart

Swim bladder

Pelvic fin for steering

Posterior dorsal fin

Liver

Anal fin

Caudal or tail fin

▲ FISH

Fish live in water and have a protective covering of scales on their outer bodies. They breathe by absorbing dissolved oxygen in the water using organs called gills located at the back of their heads. Most fish have an array of blades projecting from their body called fins. These give the fish stability in water and help control the direction of its movement.

Octopus

Starfish

Jellyfish

▲ ECHINODERMS

Starfish, sea urchins, and star dollars are all echinoderms. Their skeletons are made of chalky plates that are sometimes covered in small spines. All echinoderms' bodies are divided into five parts. Starfish, for example, all have five arms and five sets of digestive and reproductive organs. If an arm breaks off, it will grow back.

▼ CRUSTACEANS

This group of more than 40,000 species of invertebrates ranges from tiny water fleas no more than 0.1 mm in size up to the Japanese spider crab, with a leg span in excess of 13 ft (3.7 m). Crustaceans include shrimps, lobsters, and crabs. They all have hard-jointed shells, eyes on stalks, and four or more pairs of jointed legs.

▼ CNIDARIANS

Jellyfish, sea anemones, and coral are all cnidarians. These creatures have no brain or central nervous system. They tend to have a bell-shaped or hollow body and a mouth ringed with tentacles. The mouth contains stinging cells, called nematocysts, which can disable prey. Some jellyfish are harmful to humans—for example, an Australian box jellyfish sting can kill within minutes.

▼ CORAL

Coral are made up of individual, small creatures called polyps. They are part of the cnidarian group. Their vivid colors come from bright algae that grow in the coral's tissue. As coral dies, its hard outer casing falls and, over long periods of time, builds up to form coral reefs.

▲ CEPHALOPODS

Mollusks that lack a complete hard outer shell but have tentacles are known as cephalopods. These include cuttlefish, squid, and octopuses. An octopus has eight arms, a well-developed brain, and good eyesight. It can react quickly to danger, squirting out a jet of water to propel itself away.

▼ SPONGES

There are as many as 10,000 species of sponges. Sponges are simple, invertebrate creatures. They are found mostly in saltwater habitats although some freshwater species exist. Sponges attach to rocks and feed on tiny food particles that flow through openings called ostia.

▼ MOLLUSKS

Most mollusks are soft-bodied creatures covered in a shell. These shells are made from calcium carbonate secreted by a body part called the mantle. The giant clam can live for up to 100 years and can grow to more than 4 ft (1.2 m) across. However, most mollusks (including snails, oysters, and mussels) are much smaller.

Giant clam

Orange puffball

Pink sea fan coral

Crab

MAMMALS

Around 220 million years ago, mammals evolved from a group of reptiles called therapsids. Early mammals were shrewlike creatures that survived partly because their warm-blooded bodies enabled them to be active at night (nocturnal). Today, there are more than 5,000 species of mammals distributed worldwide. These range in size from the lightest, the Etruscan shrew, which weighs less than 0.07 oz (2 g), to the the heaviest, the blue whale, which weighs more than 150 tons.

❶ LIVE YOUNG

Nearly all mammals give birth to live young. Some, such as this wildebeest, can stand and move within minutes of being born. Marsupials, by contrast, are born alive but not fully developed. They are then kept safe in their mother's marsupium, or pouch, where they feed on her milk, until they are more developed. Kangaroos, koala bears, and wallabies are all marsupials.

❸ MOTHER'S MILK

Female mammals feed their newborn young on nutritious milk from their mammary glands. This milk is rich in fats and proteins that promote growth. It also contains antibodies that protect against disease. Young mammals suckle by clasping onto teats or nipples with their mouths, which open as they draw in milk. Human beings have two nipples while pigs have 16.

❹ PARENTING

Mammals are among nature's most hands-on parents. The young of many species are taught not only feeding and survival skills, but also how to behave within their social group. Meerkats live in social groups called mobs, in which the young are mentored by the adults. When meerkats forage or dig for food, they are vulnerable to attack, so one or more members of the mob keeps watch, standing on its hind legs.

Adult male giraffes can be more than 16 ft (5 m) tall

Duck-billed platypuses are one of three mammals that lay eggs

❷ MONOTREMES

Monotremes are mammal exceptions. They are the only mammals that lay eggs. Found solely in Australia and New Guinea, there are only three species of monotremes—two types of echidnas, or spiny anteaters, and the duck-billed platypus. Monotremes do not suckle. Instead they lick milk that runs over the belly of their mother.

❺ VERTEBRATES

All mammals are vertebrates. This means that their body is supported by an internal skeleton, including a backbone made of individual vertebra bones. The neck of almost all mammals contains seven vertebrae. In the case of giraffes, each of the seven vertebrae is about 10 in (25 cm) long and flexible.

❻ INSULATION

Most mammals have layers of fat underneath their skin to help insulate them from the cold. Mammals that live in colder climates often have thicker fat layers. Marine mammals, such as these walruses, which live in the Arctic, have a layer of fat called blubber that can reach thicknesses of 6 in (15 cm). An adult walrus can weigh up to 1.6 tons.

❼ FUR AND HAIR

A mammal's skin is covered in hair or fur for some or all of its life. The strands of fur and hair trap air and help keep the animal warm. The sea otter lacks the thick layer of blubber of other marine mammals, but has an extremely dense arrangement of hair. More than 40,000 hairs can be packed into a single square centimeter of its body.

A beaver's front incisor teeth can chop through tree trunks and branches

❽ WARM-BLOODED

Mammals are warm-blooded and thus are able to maintain a constant temperature. While their sweat glands release perspiration, they also adopt certain behaviors to cool down. These include resting in the shade, as the leopard above.

❾ LOWER JAW

Mammals have a single lower jawbone and most have a number of different types of teeth that are specialized for different tasks. Incisors snip and bite, canines pierce and tear, premolars slice materials, and molars crush and grind foods.

❿ SUPER SENSES

Mammals have highly developed senses. For example, the star-nosed mole has 22 tentacles around its nose. These are sensitive to touch. They enable the mole to identify insects and other prey without using sight.

ECOSYSTEMS

Ecosystems are complete communities of different living things, together with their environment including the climate. An ecosystem can be as small as a pond or a single rotting tree stump, or as large as a tropical rain forest. Ecosystems are treated as separate units since this makes them easier to chart and study. In reality, they are rarely closed systems, and food and energy may flow from one ecosystem to another.

Pond algae is a primary producer, making its food via photosynthesis

◀ FOOD CHAINS
Food chains are a simple way of describing the flow of food and energy through an ecosystem. Plants, which make their food from sunlight by photosynthesis, are known as primary producers. Animals cannot make their own food, so they must consume either these plants or creatures that eat plants. Those that eat plants are primary consumers, and they are eaten by secondary consumers. At each level of consumption, known as a trophic level, large amounts of energy consumed by one living thing are lost. Only a fraction of the energy it used is passed on when it is eaten by another creature.

▲ HABITATS
A creature's habitat is where it lives. Some animals have adapted to live in unusual habitats or to use the discarded homes of others. The elf owl often makes its home in holes in saguaro cacti, which were previously gila woodpeckers' nests.

Insect larva is a primary consumer, feeding on pond algae

Barn owl swoops in to kill and eat the snake

Frog is a secondary consumer, using rapid movement of its sticky tongue to catch larvae

Small grass snake feeds on frogs as well as insects and other pond life

◄ DECOMPOSERS

Fly agaric mushrooms grow among rotting plant matter on the forest floor. Mushrooms, toadstools, molds, and other fungi, along with bacteria and some worms, recycle dead matter through decomposition. As they feed, decomposers break down dead plant and animal matter into fibrous humus and valuable minerals and nutrients that enrich the soil.

This sea anemone is carried around on the shell of a hermit crab

◄ MUTUALISM

A relationship where both species benefit is called mutualism. For example, bees get nectar from the flowers they pollinate, and bacteria living in the guts of cows aid digestion and receive nutrients as a result. This red-billed oxpecker eats the ticks on a hippopotamus. In doing so, it acquires food while removing pests.

▲ COMMENSALISM

Many different species have close relationships with one another in an ecosystem. Commensalism is when one species benefits, while the other is not significantly harmed. Epiphytic plants, such as orchids, bromeliads, and some ferns and mosses, live on taller plants to gain more access to sunlight.

◄ PARASITISM

When one species benefits while harming another, called the host, it is known as parasitism. Aphids are parasites that feed on plants, sucking the sap from stems and foliage. They can distort a plant's growth, transmit viruses, or encourage the growth of damaging molds. Some parasites, such as tapeworms, live inside their hosts. Others are carried from one host to another, such as malaria, which is carried by mosquitoes.

► BALANCING ACT

A thriving ecosystem has a balance between producers and consumers and the environment they live in. The introduction of new species into an ecosystem is just one way that this balance can be disturbed. In 1935, just over 100 cane toads were introduced to Australia in an effort to combat beetles that ate sugar-cane crops. Cane toad numbers have since grown to more than 100 million. They are a danger to native animals with their poisonous skin and voracious feeding habits.

▼ CELLS

There are about 200 different types of cells in the body, from adipose cells, which act as stores of oils or fat, to mammary-gland cells, which can secrete milk in female breasts. Although they perform different functions, cells tend to have the same basic structure, with a nucleus and jellylike cytoplasm contained within a thin outer membrane.

The human body's building blocks are some 100 trillion cells. Many of these microscopic units are grouped together to form tissues. An organ, which performs one or more key functions, consists of two or more types of tissues and often works along with other cells, tissues, and organs in a system. The human body relies on 12 major systems, including the lymphatic system and the circulatory system.

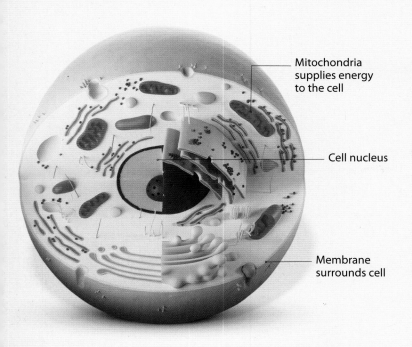

Mitochondria supplies energy to the cell

Cell nucleus

Membrane surrounds cell

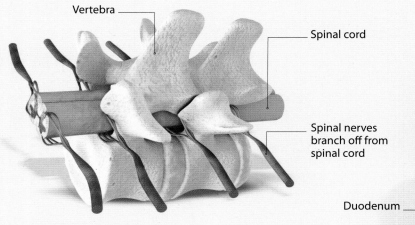

Vertebra

Spinal cord

Spinal nerves branch off from spinal cord

Duodenum

▲ NERVOUS TISSUE

Networks of long cells carry electrical signals through the body to and from the brain. In addition to individual nerves, nervous tissue forms the brain inside the skull and the spinal cord that runs through the vertebrae of the backbone.

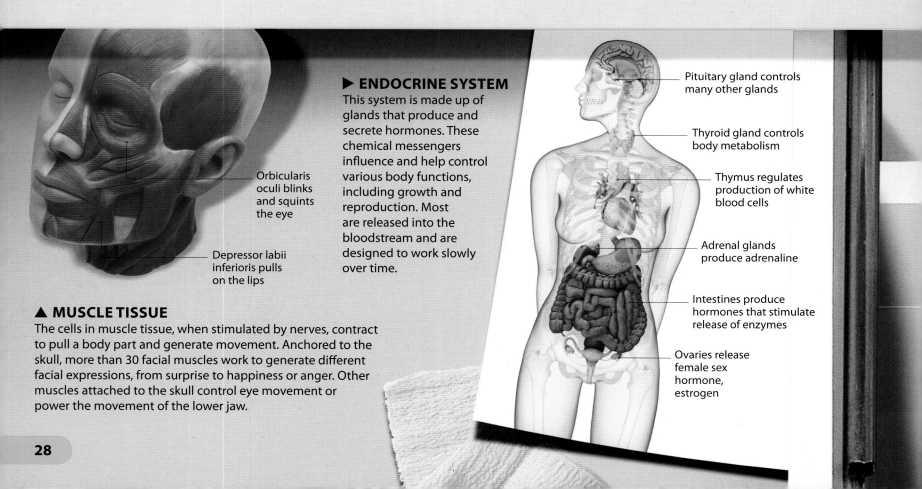

Orbicularis oculi blinks and squints the eye

Depressor labii inferioris pulls on the lips

▲ MUSCLE TISSUE

The cells in muscle tissue, when stimulated by nerves, contract to pull a body part and generate movement. Anchored to the skull, more than 30 facial muscles work to generate different facial expressions, from surprise to happiness or anger. Other muscles attached to the skull control eye movement or power the movement of the lower jaw.

▶ ENDOCRINE SYSTEM

This system is made up of glands that produce and secrete hormones. These chemical messengers influence and help control various body functions, including growth and reproduction. Most are released into the bloodstream and are designed to work slowly over time.

Pituitary gland controls many other glands

Thyroid gland controls body metabolism

Thymus regulates production of white blood cells

Adrenal glands produce adrenaline

Intestines produce hormones that stimulate release of enzymes

Ovaries release female sex hormone, estrogen

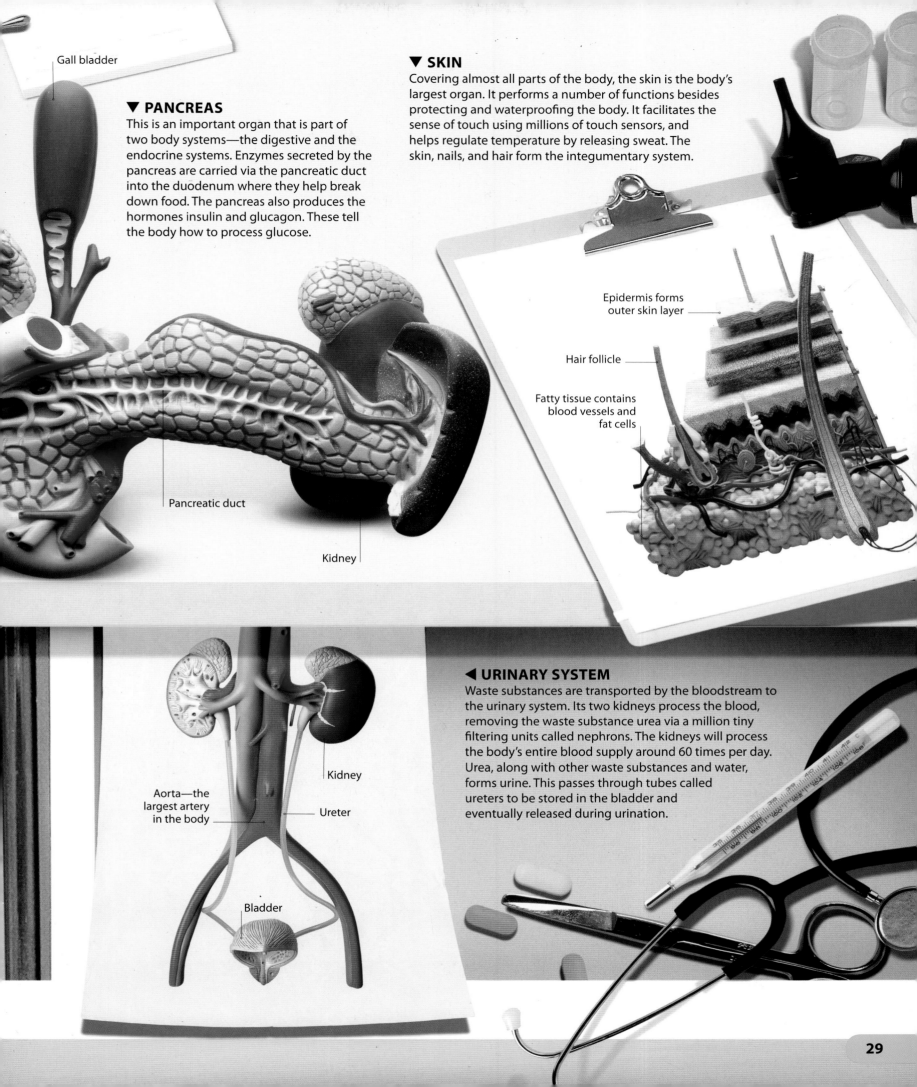

Gall bladder

▼ PANCREAS

This is an important organ that is part of two body systems—the digestive and the endocrine systems. Enzymes secreted by the pancreas are carried via the pancreatic duct into the duodenum where they help break down food. The pancreas also produces the hormones insulin and glucagon. These tell the body how to process glucose.

Pancreatic duct

Kidney

▼ SKIN

Covering almost all parts of the body, the skin is the body's largest organ. It performs a number of functions besides protecting and waterproofing the body. It facilitates the sense of touch using millions of touch sensors, and helps regulate temperature by releasing sweat. The skin, nails, and hair form the integumentary system.

Epidermis forms outer skin layer

Hair follicle

Fatty tissue contains blood vessels and fat cells

Kidney

◄ URINARY SYSTEM

Waste substances are transported by the bloodstream to the urinary system. Its two kidneys process the blood, removing the waste substance urea via a million tiny filtering units called nephrons. The kidneys will process the body's entire blood supply around 60 times per day. Urea, along with other waste substances and water, forms urine. This passes through tubes called ureters to be stored in the bladder and eventually released during urination.

Aorta—the largest artery in the body

Ureter

Bladder

SKELETON AND MUSCLES

The human body has 206 lightweight but strong bones. They provide protection, support, and a framework that anchors the body's many muscles. Bones range in size from the tiny stapes in your ear to your femur or thighbone, which is the longest. Some, such as the ribs that form the rib cage, and the skull, act as protective bowls or cages for delicate internal organs.

▶ SKELETON

The skeleton can be divided into two parts—the axial and the appendicular. The axial skeleton consists of the skull, the vertebral column, the ribs, and the sternum or breastbone at the front of the chest. The appendicular skeleton is the bones in the arms and legs as well as the shoulder and hip girdles, which attach the limbs to the axial skeleton.

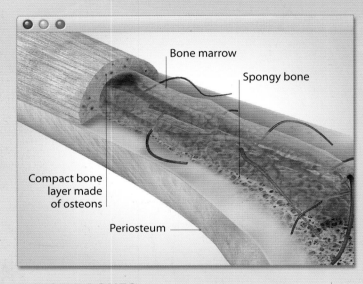

Bone marrow

Spongy bone

Compact bone layer made of osteons

Periosteum

▲ INSIDE BONES

This cutaway of the humerus (upper arm bone) shows the hard compact bone layer made of tubes called osteons and a lighter layer called spongy bone. At the center is bone marrow, which in long bones stores fat and in some flat bones, such as ribs, makes new red blood cells. Blood vessels provide the bone with nutrients and oxygen.

Cranium or skull

Cervical vertebrae form top of spine

Radius

Humerus

Ribs form protective rib cage

Ulna

Coccyx (tailbone)

Pelvis

Femur runs from knee up to hip socket

Fibula

Tibia or shin bone

Patella or kneecap

Heel bone called calcaneus

Tarsal bones

Phalanges (toe bones)

Metatarsal bones link phalanges to tarsals

▶ SYNOVIAL JOINTS

Joints are the points at which two or more bones meet. Synovial joints, such as the knee, offer large amounts of movement. The ends of the bones are covered in cartilage and separated by a cavity filled with synovial fluid, which reduces friction.

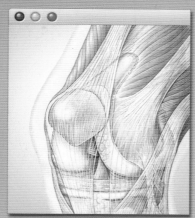

▼ RANGE OF MOVEMENT

Some bone joints are immovable, such as the plates that form the skull, or are slightly flexible, such as the vertebrae in the spine. Others are extremely flexible. The joints in the fingers and hands allow us to grasp large objects or manipulate small ones.

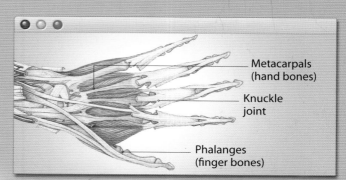

Metacarpals (hand bones)

Knuckle joint

Phalanges (finger bones)

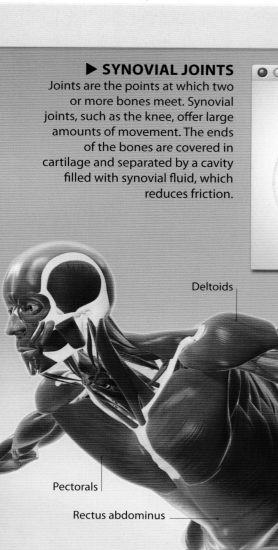

Deltoids

Triceps

Biceps

Pectorals

Rectus abdominus

Quadriceps (thigh muscle)

Gluteus maximus

Hamstrings

Gastrocnemius (calf muscle)

Achilles tendon

Flexor digitorum brevis

◀ MUSCLES

The human body has three types of muscles. Cardiac muscle is found in the heart. Smooth muscle is found inside organs, such as the intestines. Skeletal muscles cover the skeleton, giving the body its shape, and are connected to bones by cords called tendons.

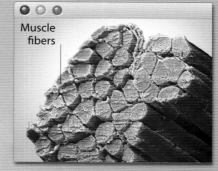

Muscle fibers

▲ SKELETAL MUSCLES

Skeletal muscles are full of long fibers containing tiny strands called myrofibrils. Blood vessels run through muscles, supplying oxygen and nutrients, while nerve endings carry impulses from the brain and central nervous system. Muscle cells contract in response to nerve signals.

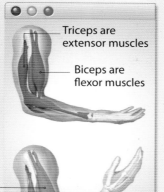

Triceps are extensor muscles

Biceps are flexor muscles

Biceps contract, pulling forearm upward

◀ MUSCLE MOVEMENT

Muscles perform work by contracting and pulling a body part in one direction. Muscles cannot push, so an opposing muscle group is required to pull the body part back to its original position. Muscles that bend a joint are called flexors and those that straighten it are called extensors.

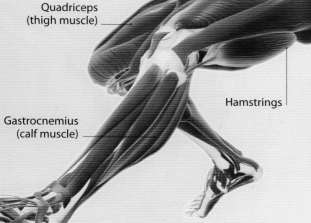

BLOOD AND BREATHING

Every second, the circulatory system delivers oxygen and nutrients to body cells. At the center of the system is the heart, a muscular pump that drives blood around the body through a massive network of blood vessels. If laid end to end, these would stretch a distance of 93,000 miles (150,000 km). This network is divided into arteries, which transport blood away from the heart, and veins, which carry blood back to the heart.

Subclavian vein carries blood from arms

Subclavian artery carries blood to arms

Heart

Femoral artery carries blood to legs

Femoral vein transports blood from legs

Anterior tibial artery carries blood to lower leg and foot

Great saphenous vein carries blood from foot

◀ THERE AND BACK
Blood travels twice through the heart on each cycle of its journey around the body. Deoxygenated (oxygen-poor) blood is carried back from the body to the heart in veins. It is then pumped into the lungs. There, gas exchange takes place and the resulting oxygen-rich blood travels back into the heart, before it is pumped out through arteries around the body.

▼ BLOOD COMPOSITION
A human body contains about 9–11 pints (5–6 liters) of blood. Blood consists of a liquid called plasma and three types of cells. Red cells are oxygen-carriers, while white cells fight diseases. Small cell fragments called platelets clump together to seal leaks in blood vessels when damage occurs.

▲ BLOOD
Blood is the body's delivery system. It carries chemical hormones, infection-fighting cells and antibodies, and many other crucial substances. Blood plasma transports dissolved food and nutrients around the body in addition to carrying waste substances away. Red blood cells contain hemoglobin, which transports oxygen to and waste carbon dioxide away from body cells. A red blood cell can carry one billion oxygen molecules.

▼ THE HEART
The heart is divided into four chambers—a right and left atrium and two lower ventricles. A human heart beats on average about 70–75 times per minute, and will pump blood an estimated 2.5 billion times in a person's lifetime. The muscular walls of the atria and ventricles contract to push blood through and out of the heart.

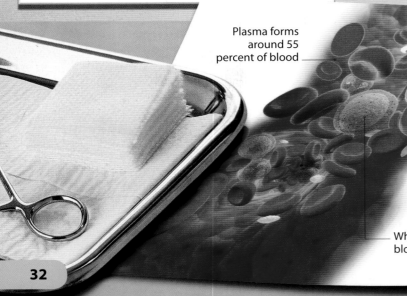

Plasma forms around 55 percent of blood

Platelet

Red blood cells form almost 45 percent of blood

White blood cell

Superior vena cava carries deoxygenated blood to the heart

Pulmonary artery carries deoxygenated blood to lungs

Aorta carries blood to body

Right atrium pushes blood into aorta

Right ventricle pushes blood into right atrium

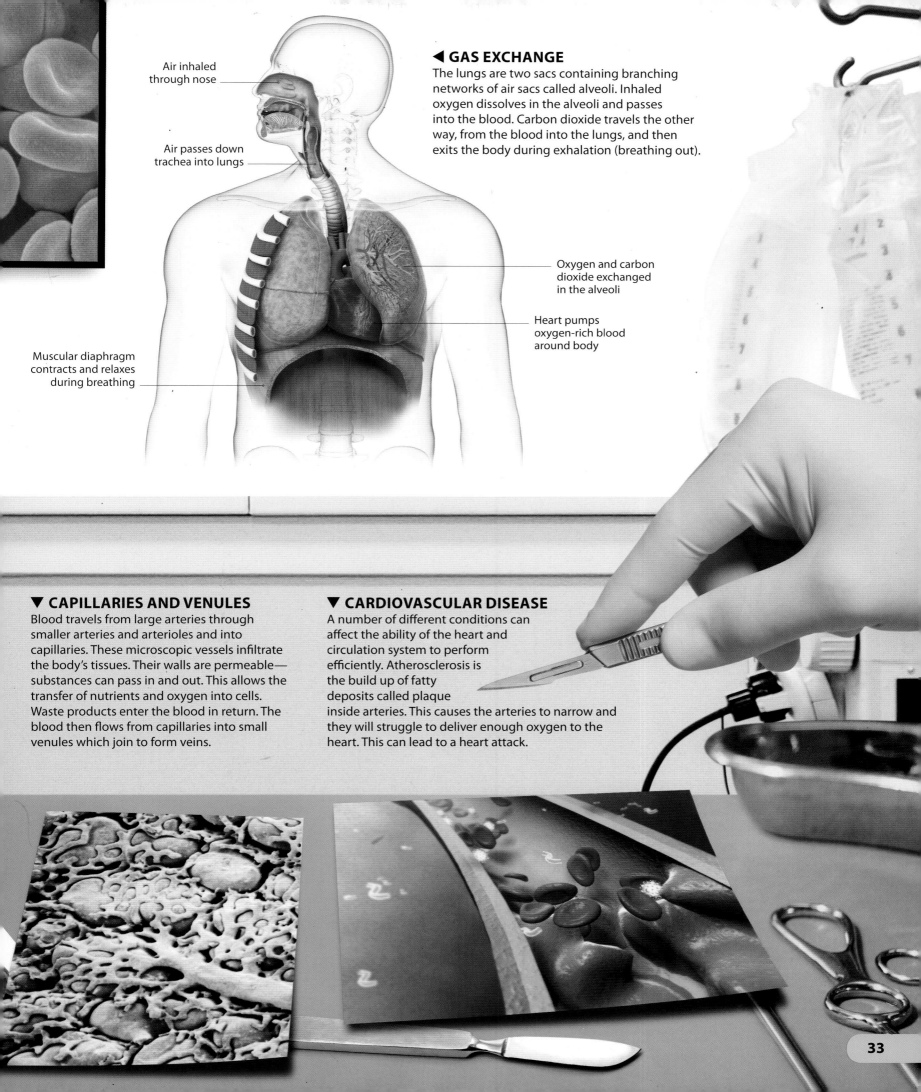

◄ GAS EXCHANGE

The lungs are two sacs containing branching networks of air sacs called alveoli. Inhaled oxygen dissolves in the alveoli and passes into the blood. Carbon dioxide travels the other way, from the blood into the lungs, and then exits the body during exhalation (breathing out).

Air inhaled through nose

Air passes down trachea into lungs

Muscular diaphragm contracts and relaxes during breathing

Oxygen and carbon dioxide exchanged in the alveoli

Heart pumps oxygen-rich blood around body

▼ CAPILLARIES AND VENULES

Blood travels from large arteries through smaller arteries and arterioles and into capillaries. These microscopic vessels infiltrate the body's tissues. Their walls are permeable—substances can pass in and out. This allows the transfer of nutrients and oxygen into cells. Waste products enter the blood in return. The blood then flows from capillaries into small venules which join to form veins.

▼ CARDIOVASCULAR DISEASE

A number of different conditions can affect the ability of the heart and circulation system to perform efficiently. Atherosclerosis is the build up of fatty deposits called plaque inside arteries. This causes the arteries to narrow and they will struggle to deliver enough oxygen to the heart. This can lead to a heart attack.

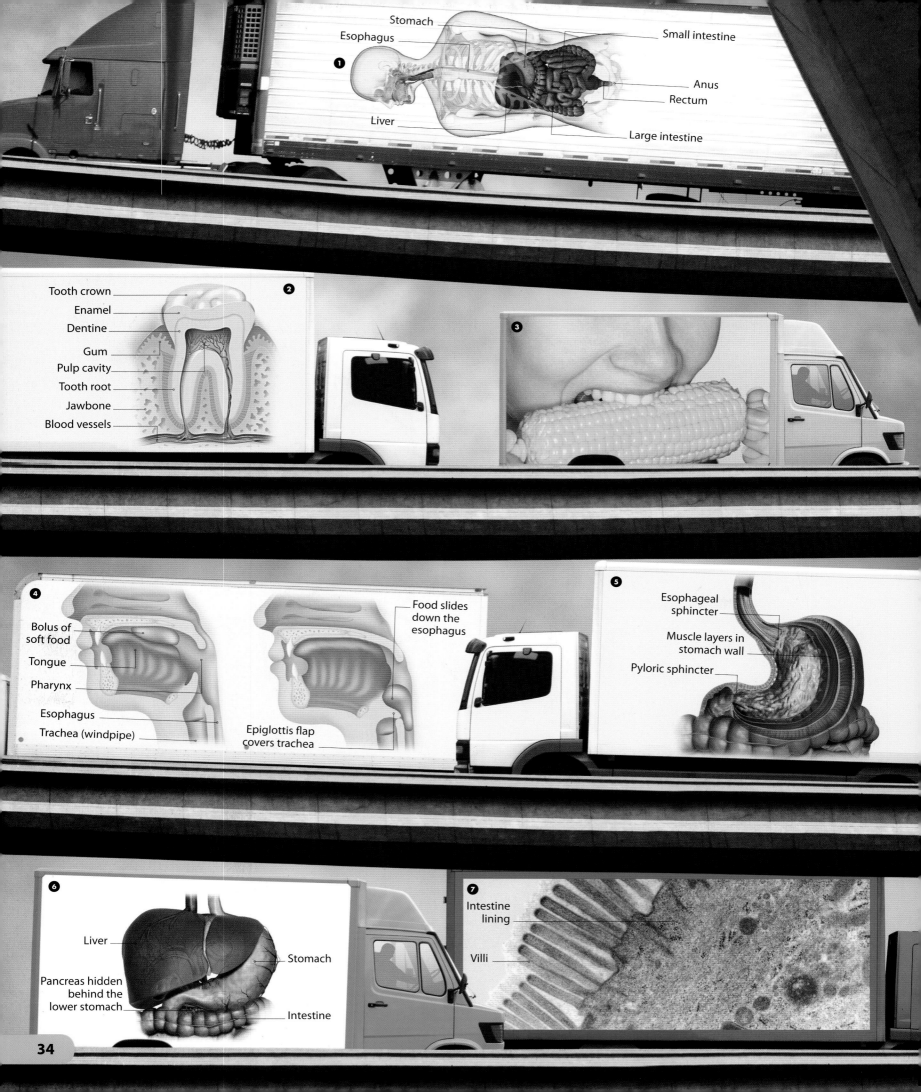

1

Esophagus
Stomach
Small intestine
Anus
Rectum
Large intestine
Liver

2

Tooth crown
Enamel
Dentine
Gum
Pulp cavity
Tooth root
Jawbone
Blood vessels

3

4

Bolus of soft food
Tongue
Pharynx
Esophagus
Trachea (windpipe)
Epiglottis flap covers trachea
Food slides down the esophagus

5

Esophageal sphincter
Muscle layers in stomach wall
Pyloric sphincter

6

Liver
Pancreas hidden behind the lower stomach
Stomach
Intestine

7

Intestine lining
Villi

THE DIGESTIVE SYSTEM

The nutrients the human body needs from food are locked up in large food molecules. Digestion is the process of breaking down food into substances that can be absorbed by the bloodstream and cells. Once in the cells, the energy and nutrients from food are used as fuel for movement, and cell and tissue growth and repair. The digestion process begins even before food enters the mouth, with the smell of it stimulating the salivary glands.

❶ DIGESTIVE SYSTEM

The digestive system in humans is about 30 ft (9 m) long and is called the alimentary canal. Food takes 24 hours or longer to complete a journey that begins in the mouth and ends with waste matter being passed out of the anus opening. Along the way, food is broken down by different parts of the digestive system before it is absorbed.

❷ TAKE A BITE

An adult human has 32 teeth in the gums and jawbones. The crown of the tooth (the part above the gum) is covered in a hard layer of enamel that protects the bonelike dentine underneath. Front incisor teeth cut and slice food, while the blocklike molars at the back grind the food down.

❸ CHEWING

The lips and front teeth pull food inside the mouth where cheek muscles drive the jaws in a chewing motion. The muscular tongue presses food against the teeth. Three pairs of ducts inject saliva, which lubricates the food as it is crushed. It also contains the enzyme ptyalin, which begins to break down starch in the food.

❹ SWALLOWING

Once the food is a soft, moist mass called a bolus, it is pushed to the pharynx at the back of the mouth by the tongue and enters the esophagus. This muscular tube contracts and relaxes in a wavelike sequence called peristalsis, which carries the food on a six-second journey to the stomach.

❺ IN THE STOMACH

The stomach expands to accept food through a ring of muscle called the esophageal sphincter. Layers of muscle in the stomach's walls contract about three times per minute to crush and churn food. The stomach makes gastric juices that contain enzymes that break down the food. At the other end of the stomach, the pyloric sphincter stops food from entering the intestines.

❻ LIVER AND PANCREAS

The stomach content, called chyme, is stored for two to six hours. After this, the pyloric sphincter opens and the chyme is pushed into the small intestine. Here, the chyme is made less acidic, while bile from the liver breaks down fats, making them easier to digest. Pancreatic juice breaks down food into simpler units.

❼ SMALL INTESTINE

Enzymes continue their work in the small intestine. Its walls are covered in vast numbers of fingerlike projections called villi, which absorb food. Proteins are changed into amino acids, fats into fatty acids, and carbohydrates into sugars. These now pass through the walls of the intestine into the bloodstream.

❽ LARGE INTESTINE

The watery remains of undigested food and juices leave the small intestine and enter the 5–6 ft (1.5–1.8 m) long large intestine, where they spend 12 to 24 hours. Here, large amounts of water and some minerals are absorbed, while more than 400 different types of bacteria, such as these saccharolytic bacteria, break down and absorb additional nutrients. The remaining matter, called feces, is stored in the rectum and pushed out of the anus.

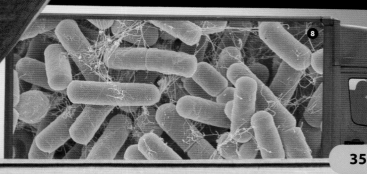

8

BRAIN AND SENSES

Humans rely on their senses to obtain information about the world around them. Data from the sensory organs continually bombards the brain. This organ monitors and regulates the body's unconscious actions, such as breathing and digestion, as well as conscious thought and movement. The brain sends instructions and receives sensory information as electrical signals via the nervous system.

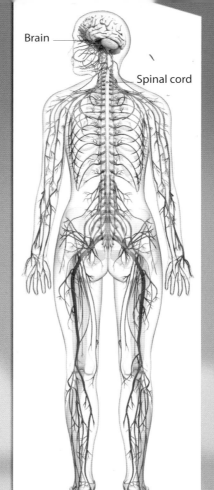

Brain

Spinal cord

▼ THE BRAIN
The brain is the body's control center. Weighing about 3.5 lb (1.5 kg), it consumes more than 20 percent of the body's energy as it receives feedback from the body's senses. It also makes decisions and sends instructions to the rest of the body. The brain consists of about 100 billion brain cells called neurons, which form enormous networks with each other.

▶ THE NERVOUS SYSTEM
The central nervous system consists of the brain and spinal cord. Branching off are the many millions of neurons that form the peripheral nervous system, which extends throughout the body. Sensory neurons carry information to the central nervous system, while motor neurons carry instructions from the central nervous system to move muscles.

TOUCH ▼
The sense of touch provides data about the body's immediate surroundings. Different receptors in the skin respond to light touch, pressure, vibrations, temperature, and pain. The receptors are all over the body, but they are not distributed evenly. Certain parts, such as the lips and fingertips, are more sensitive since they contain a great number of receptors.

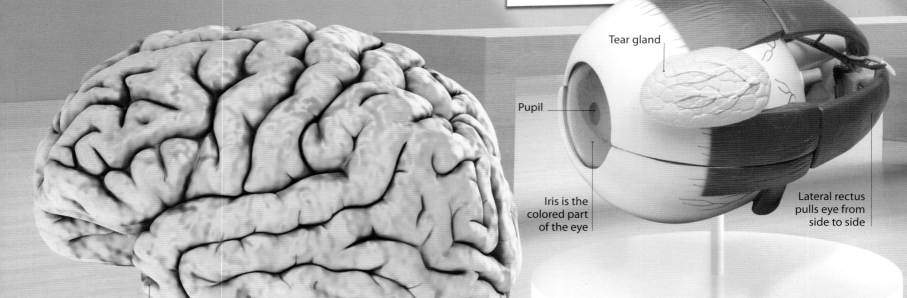

Superior rectus muscle rolls eye upward

Tear gland

Pupil

Iris is the colored part of the eye

Lateral rectus pulls eye from side to side

Cerebrum is the brain's key decision-making area

Pons carries signals from the forebrain to the cerebellum

Spinal cord

Cerebellum coordinates muscle movement and balance

▲ SIGHT
Eyeballs are protected by a bony socket, with tear ducts to wash the eyeball's surface every few seconds. Light enters the eye through the clear cornea and an opening called the pupil. A lens focuses the light so it falls on the retina at the back of the eye. The retina contains millions of photoreceptor cells. These are rods, which "see" in black and white, or cones, which "see" in color.

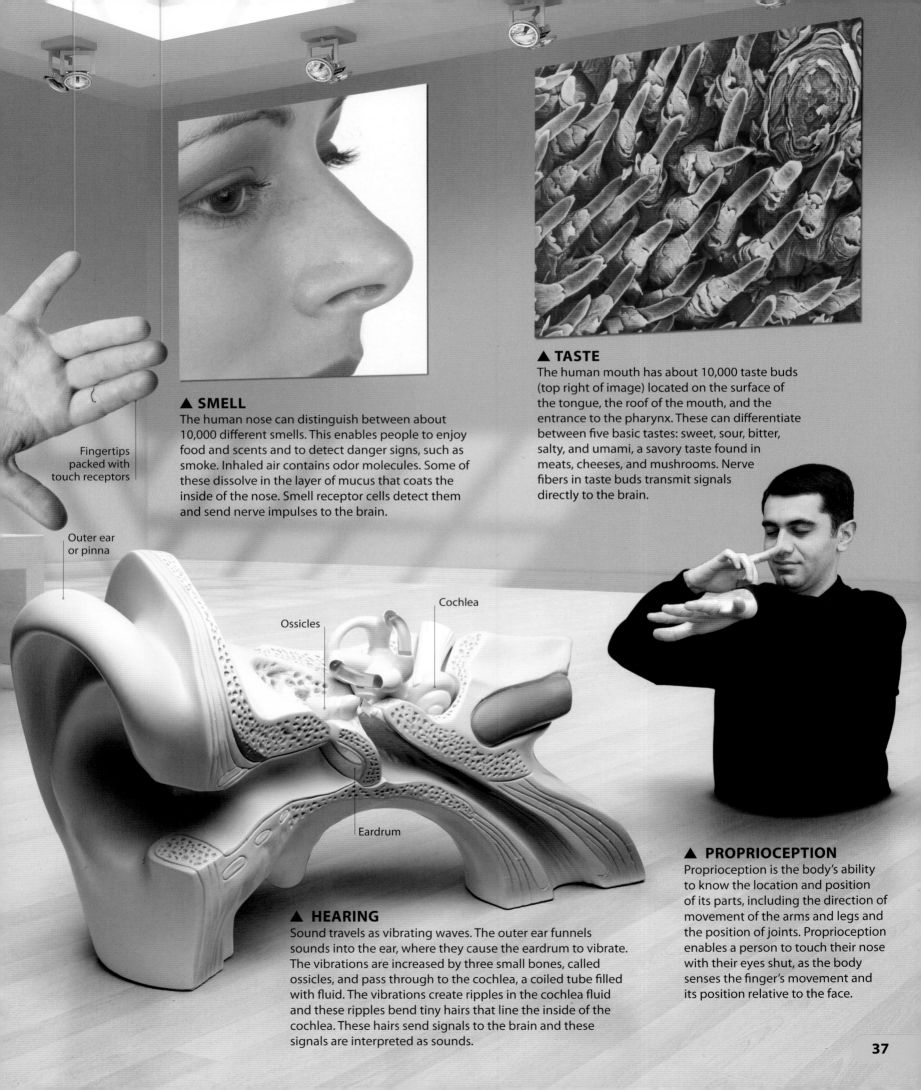

▲ SMELL

The human nose can distinguish between about 10,000 different smells. This enables people to enjoy food and scents and to detect danger signs, such as smoke. Inhaled air contains odor molecules. Some of these dissolve in the layer of mucus that coats the inside of the nose. Smell receptor cells detect them and send nerve impulses to the brain.

▲ TASTE

The human mouth has about 10,000 taste buds (top right of image) located on the surface of the tongue, the roof of the mouth, and the entrance to the pharynx. These can differentiate between five basic tastes: sweet, sour, bitter, salty, and umami, a savory taste found in meats, cheeses, and mushrooms. Nerve fibers in taste buds transmit signals directly to the brain.

Fingertips packed with touch receptors

Outer ear or pinna

Cochlea

Ossicles

Eardrum

▲ HEARING

Sound travels as vibrating waves. The outer ear funnels sounds into the ear, where they cause the eardrum to vibrate. The vibrations are increased by three small bones, called ossicles, and pass through to the cochlea, a coiled tube filled with fluid. The vibrations create ripples in the cochlea fluid and these ripples bend tiny hairs that line the inside of the cochlea. These hairs send signals to the brain and these signals are interpreted as sounds.

▲ PROPRIOCEPTION

Proprioception is the body's ability to know the location and position of its parts, including the direction of movement of the arms and legs and the position of joints. Proprioception enables a person to touch their nose with their eyes shut, as the body senses the finger's movement and its position relative to the face.

37

BODY REPAIR

The human body has a remarkable capacity for regrowth, repair, and regeneration. Processes within the body help sustain and maintain many of its parts during life. In an adult human, somatic stem cells are unspecialized cells that can be harnessed by the body and turned into certain types of blood, bone, or nerve cells. When the human body cannot repair a body part, medical science has found ways to help.

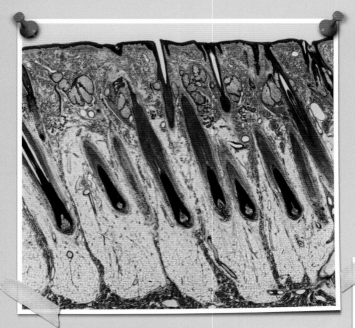

▲ CONSTANT REPLACEMENT

Some types of cells in the human body are replaced in a continual process. Red blood cells last a matter of months before being replaced, while human liver cells are regenerated every 300–500 days. Cells on the skin's surface (pictured above) rub and flake off steadily. They are replaced by cells in the deepest layer of the epidermis. These divide into new cells, are pushed toward the surface, die, and form a protective barrier.

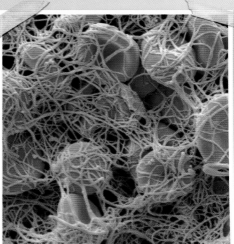

◀ HEALING WOUNDS

When a cut occurs, red blood cells clump together with a mesh of a protein called fibrin (shown as gray fibers), forming a clot. Wounds can allow harmful substances into the body. Some white blood cells produce antibodies that fight any infection caused by these substances. Others perform the process of phagocytosis—surrounding and consuming bacteria. Blood capillaries grow into the area and, over time, new tissue forms around and over the wound.

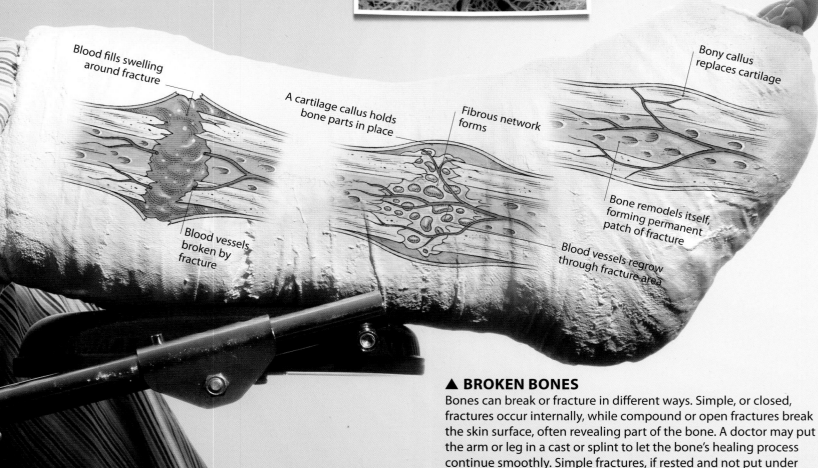

Blood fills swelling around fracture

A cartilage callus holds bone parts in place

Fibrous network forms

Bony callus replaces cartilage

Blood vessels broken by fracture

Bone remodels itself, forming permanent patch of fracture

Blood vessels regrow through fracture area

▲ BROKEN BONES

Bones can break or fracture in different ways. Simple, or closed, fractures occur internally, while compound or open fractures break the skin surface, often revealing part of the bone. A doctor may put the arm or leg in a cast or splint to let the bone's healing process continue smoothly. Simple fractures, if rested and not put under strain, usually take five to eight weeks to heal.

▼ ▶ REPLACEMENT JOINTS

Wear and tear, injury, or disease can all seriously affect the smooth working of load-bearing joints, such as the hip, knee, or ankle. The joint cartilage, which reduces friction between the moving bones, can wear away, causing pain, swelling, and lack of movement. Major surgery can replace the natural joint with artificial parts.

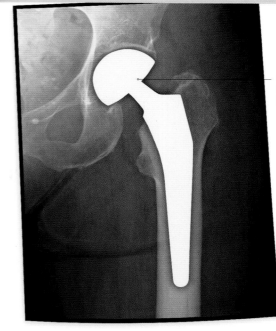

Artificial hip joint with ball fitted into hip socket

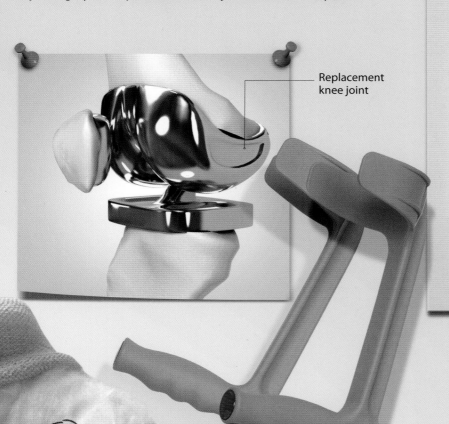

Replacement knee joint

PROSTHESES ▼

An artificial substitute for a damaged, diseased, or missing body part is called a prosthesis. Modern prosthetic arms and legs offer wearers high levels of function and mobility. South African track athlete Oscar Pistorius wears prosthetic legs made of carbon fiber, which flex on impact with the track.

◀ TRANSPLANTS

Living tissue and organs can be surgically removed from one person (the donor) and transplanted into the body of another. Some transplant organs, including hearts, are from healthy donors who died suddenly. Others, such as a single kidney, can be taken from a living donor. In all cases, drugs to suppress the body's natural defenses are required to help prevent the body from rejecting the transplant.

GENETICS

Genetics is the scientific study of genes—the instructions that govern a person's growth, development, and health. These are passed down from parents to children via sexual reproduction. Each cell in the human body has more than 20,000 genes stored in its nucleus. They provide the entire genetic code for a person and vary so that, except for identical twins, each person has slightly different genes and has their own unique set of features.

▲ CHROMOSOMES

DNA is packaged into 23 pairs of chromosomes inside a cell. Twenty-two of these pairs are similar in men and women. The 23rd pair is the sex chromosomes. These consist of two X chromosomes in females (XX) and one X and one Y chromosome in males (XY). Male and female sex cells (sperm and eggs) contain just one of the two sex chromosomes. A male child develops if the sperm contains the Y chromosome.

Chromosome forms four-armed shape just before a cell divides

▶ DNA

Genes are contained within long, ribbonlike strands of deoxyribonucleic acid (DNA) molecules. Pairs of DNA molecules wind around in what is called a double helix. They are linked by chemical substances called bases, which are found in pairs. Long sequences of base pairs form genes. DNA can copy itself when cell division occurs so that a precise copy of the DNA is present in the new cell.

▲ INHERITANCE

Three generations of the same family share many similar features as a result of a parent and child sharing 99.95 percent of their DNA. Children inherit half of their chromosomes from their father and half from their mother. Sometimes, the genes from each parent, such as hair color, do not match. In these cases, the dominant gene wins and is inherited by the child.

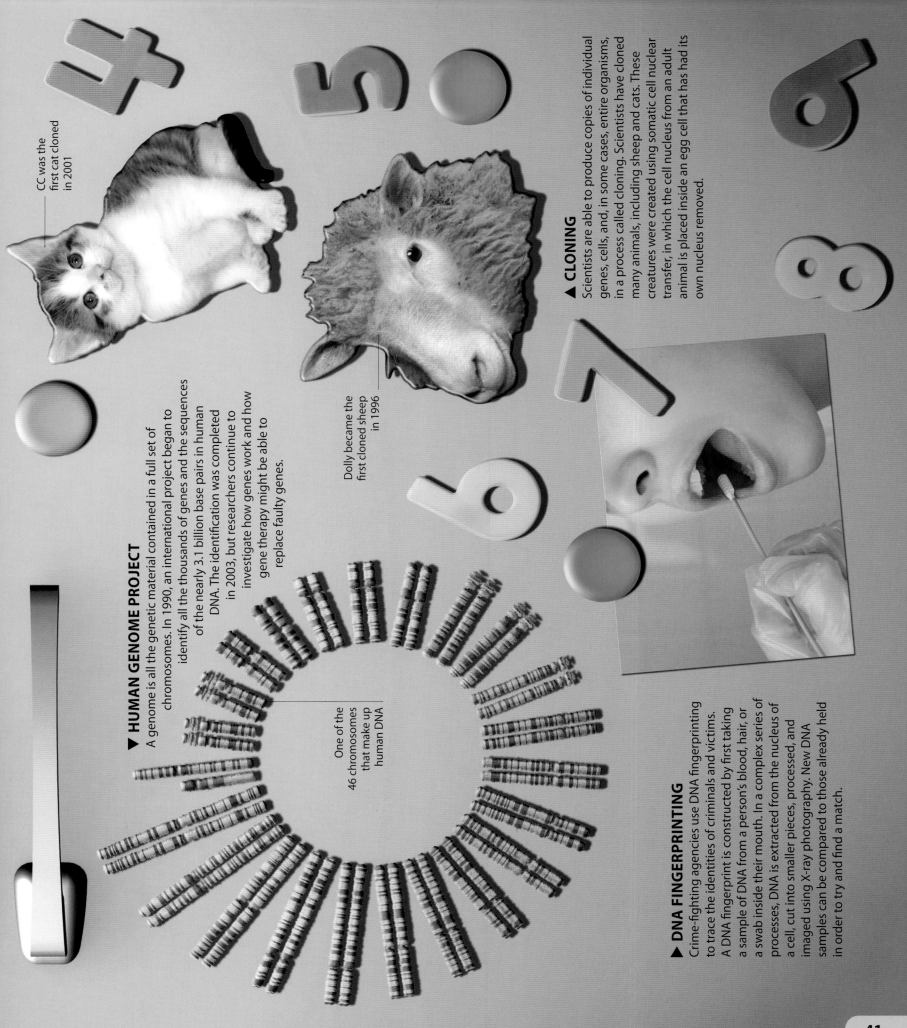

CC was the first cat cloned in 2001

▶ **HUMAN GENOME PROJECT**
A genome is all the genetic material contained in a full set of chromosomes. In 1990, an international project began to identify all the thousands of genes and the sequences of the nearly 3.1 billion base pairs in human DNA. The identification was completed in 2003, but researchers continue to investigate how genes work and how gene therapy might be able to replace faulty genes.

One of the 46 chromosomes that make up human DNA

Dolly became the first cloned sheep in 1996

▲ **CLONING**
Scientists are able to produce copies of individual genes, cells, and, in some cases, entire organisms, in a process called cloning. Scientists have cloned many animals, including sheep and cats. These creatures were created using somatic cell nuclear transfer, in which the cell nucleus from an adult animal is placed inside an egg cell that has had its own nucleus removed.

▶ **DNA FINGERPRINTING**
Crime-fighting agencies use DNA fingerprinting to trace the identities of criminals and victims. A DNA fingerprint is constructed by first taking a sample of DNA from a person's blood, hair, or a swab inside their mouth. In a complex series of processes, DNA is extracted from the nucleus of a cell, cut into smaller pieces, processed, and imaged using X-ray photography. New DNA samples can be compared to those already held in order to try and find a match.

SPIKES OF ROCK
These rock formations are called hoodoos and are found at Bryce Canyon National Park in Utah. The spires of sedimentary rock have been created over millions of years of erosion.

Earth

EARTH'S ORIGINS

Earth is around 4.6 billion years old. It is a slightly squashed sphere, measuring 7,973 miles (12,756 km) in diameter at the equator—the line running around the planet's middle at an equal distance from the North and South Poles. The planet spins on its axis and makes a complete revolution once every 23 hours and 56 minutes. Earth is the only planet in the Universe that is known to support life.

▼ EARTH FORMATION

Around 5 billion years ago, the Sun began life as a protostar, pulling dust and gas into its center, becoming hotter, and then sending out a swirling mass of gas and dust. Over hundreds of millions of years, these materials grouped together, collided, heated, and cooled to form the objects found in the Solar System, including Earth.

❶ Dust and rock Dust grains and small pieces of rock orbiting the Sun were pulled together by their own gravity. Heat generated by the collisions welded the rock together, forming larger clumps. This process is called accretion.

❷ Ball of fire Early Earth was bombarded with rocky debris, generating intense heat. This, along with radioactive reactions, melted the planet and helped create its different layers.

❸ Cooling crust Heavier, iron-rich materials moved towards the center of Earth, forming its core. Lighter materials began to cool and form the planet's mantle and outer crust.

❹ Seas and oceans The cooling Earth allowed water vapor released into the planet's early atmosphere to fall back to the surface to form early oceans.

❺ Moving land The continental crust once formed a single giant land mass called Pangaea. Around 200 million years ago, the separate continents that we know today were formed.

❻ The planet today Earth today has an oxygen-rich atmosphere and other conditions capable of supporting a huge diversity of life.

▼ INSIDE EARTH

Earth consists of three main layers—the core, the mantle, and the rocky crust. The core is divided into a solid inner core, made of iron and nickel, and a molten outer core. Temperatures in the inner core may exceed 11,900°F (6,600°C). The mantle surrounds the core, and is made up mostly of heavy, dark rock called peridotite. The crust insulates most of the surface from the very high temperatures found in the core and mantle.

Inner core is 815 miles (1,300 km) in diameter

Outer core is roughly 1,400 miles (2,200 km) thick

Mantle is 1,800 miles (2,900 km) deep

Oceanic crust is up to 3 miles (5 km) in depth

▲ LIFE ON EARTH

Precisely how life began on Earth remains unclear. It is believed, however, that life started after the planet had cooled enough for bodies of water to form. Scientists have found fossilized single-celled microorganisms in rocks that date to approximately 3.5 billion years ago. This cyanobacterium is an example of the blue-green algae bacteria thought to be one of the earliest forms of life.

▼ BUBBLING UNDER

In certain areas, water descends deep into the crust where it is heated by contact with hot rocks. Much of the water remains in geothermal reservoirs below the surface. Some, however, circulates back to the surface, forming thermal springs and jets of hot water and steam called geysers. Here, a group of Japanese macaque monkeys obtains welcome relief from the cold winter by bathing in a hot spring.

Troposphere

Stratosphere

Exosphere

▼ ATMOSPHERE

Earth's atmosphere is a cocoon of gases that surrounds the planet and extends upward, with the outer layer, the exosphere, merging into outer space. The closest layer, the troposphere, extends from sea level up to an altitude of around 10 miles (15 km). It contains circulating air and moisture, which creates most of the planet's weather. Above that is the drier stratosphere, which extends up to 30–40 miles (50–60 km).

PLATES AND FAULTS

Earth's crust is not one single piece. It is made up of a number of gigantic slabs, called plates, which float on the surface of the mantle. Heat generated by radioactivity deep within the Earth causes convection currents to run through the mantle. The plates glide on these currents, moving 0.5–8 in (1–20 cm) per year. They come together or pull apart, generating volcanic and earthquake activity and creating new landforms.

▼ CONTINENTAL DRIFT

In the distant past, the continents were in very different locations. Around 250 million years ago, they were all clumped together as one supercontinent called Pangaea. The different plates of crust then moved apart in stages in a process called continental drift. North America, for example, separated from Europe as the Atlantic Ocean started to form around 150 million years ago.

170 million years ago, South America and Africa were slowly drifting apart

Today, the Atlantic Ocean is widening at a rate of about 1 in (2.5 cm) per year

Lava spews up at Krafla in Iceland, which lies on the mid-Atlantic ocean ridge

▶ OCEAN SPREAD

New oceanic crust is created at giant rifts in the middle of the oceans, called mid-ocean ridges. As plates pull apart, pressure beneath the oceanic crust decreases, allowing molten rock (magma) from deep in Earth's mantle to rise toward the surface. Vast mountain and volcano chains form on the ocean floor, some of which may emerge above the ocean's surface as islands.

◀ PLATE BOUNDARIES

Boundaries are where two or more plates meet. At divergent boundaries, plates pull apart. At subduction boundaries, one plate slips underneath another. Transform boundaries see the plates slide and grind past each other. At collisional boundaries, two continental crust plates crunch into one another. Rock is often driven upward at boundaries to form mountain ranges. The Himalayas are formed by the collision of the Eurasian and Indo-Australian plates.

Subduction

Transform

Collisional

Divergent

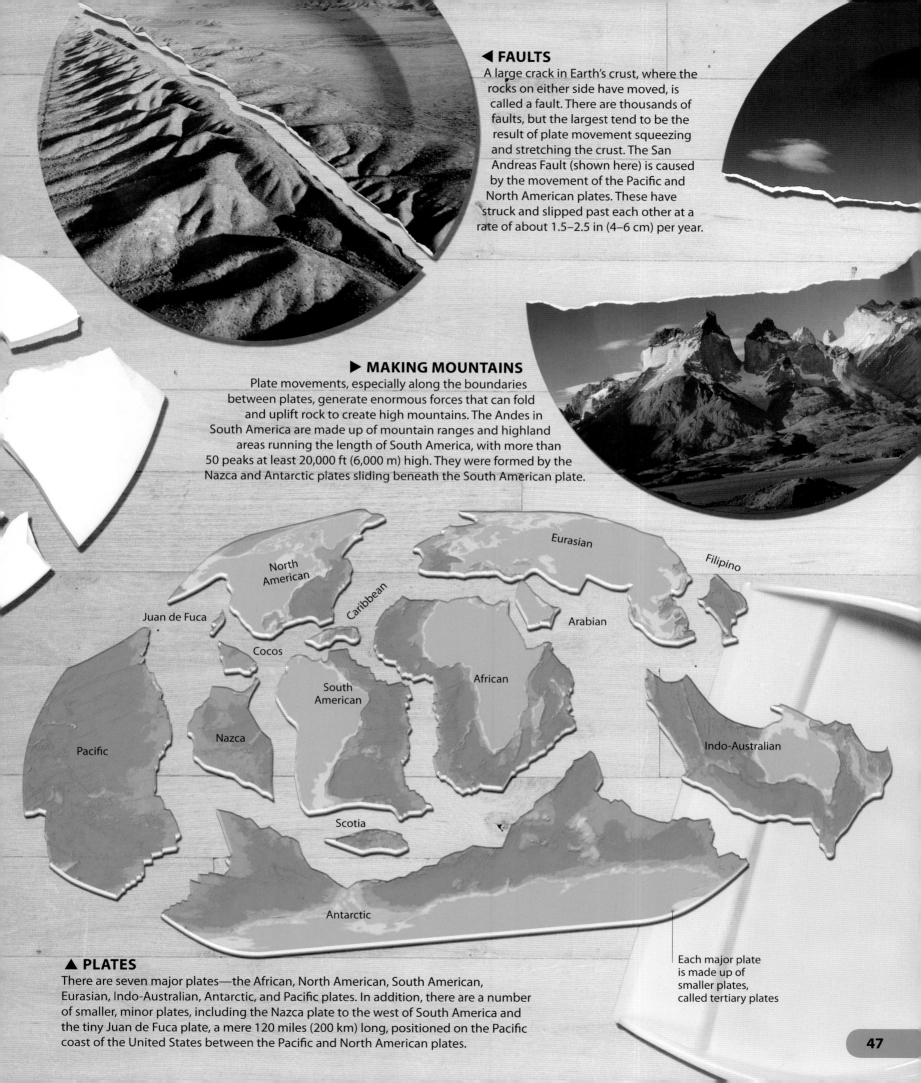

◀ FAULTS

A large crack in Earth's crust, where the rocks on either side have moved, is called a fault. There are thousands of faults, but the largest tend to be the result of plate movement squeezing and stretching the crust. The San Andreas Fault (shown here) is caused by the movement of the Pacific and North American plates. These have struck and slipped past each other at a rate of about 1.5–2.5 in (4–6 cm) per year.

▶ MAKING MOUNTAINS

Plate movements, especially along the boundaries between plates, generate enormous forces that can fold and uplift rock to create high mountains. The Andes in South America are made up of mountain ranges and highland areas running the length of South America, with more than 50 peaks at least 20,000 ft (6,000 m) high. They were formed by the Nazca and Antarctic plates sliding beneath the South American plate.

North American

Eurasian

Filipino

Juan de Fuca

Caribbean

Arabian

Cocos

African

South American

Pacific

Nazca

Indo-Australian

Scotia

Antarctic

Each major plate is made up of smaller plates, called tertiary plates

▲ PLATES

There are seven major plates—the African, North American, South American, Eurasian, Indo-Australian, Antarctic, and Pacific plates. In addition, there are a number of smaller, minor plates, including the Nazca plate to the west of South America and the tiny Juan de Fuca plate, a mere 120 miles (200 km) long, positioned on the Pacific coast of the United States between the Pacific and North American plates.

EARTHQUAKES AND VOLCANOES

Volcanoes and earthquakes tend to happen most where Earth's crust is under enormous stress, including places where plates grind up against each other, plates pull apart, or one plate subducts, sliding underneath another. Earthquakes usually occur near faults, where the movement of rocks leads to a great buildup of energy. A sudden release of this energy causes waves to travel through the crust, reaching the surface as powerful tremors.

Focus

Epicenter

◀ QUAKE!

An earthquake begins at a point underground called the hypocenter or focus. The released energy radiates outward in a series of seismic waves. These weaken in strength the farther they travel. As they move, the waves distort the rocks as they release their energy. An earthquake may be followed by additional tremors called aftershocks.

▶ EPICENTER

The point on the surface directly above the focus is called the epicenter. This is usually the area at the surface where the greatest force of the quake is felt. Major quakes can be devastating. The earthquake that struck Haiti in 2010 killed more than 220,000 people.

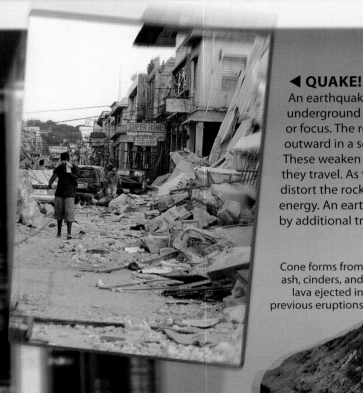

Cone forms from ash, cinders, and lava ejected in previous eruptions

◀ VOLCANIC ACTIVITY

Beneath the Earth's surface, molten rock, called magma, can form in reservoirs called magma chambers. Less dense than the surrounding rock, the magma rises and, if enough pressure builds, may reach the surface through weak areas of the crust. These volcanic eruptions vary from a gentle oozing above ground to explosive eruptions.

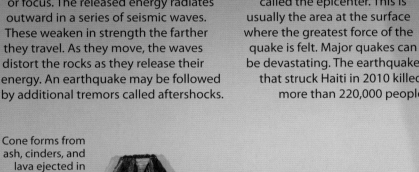

Magma chamber

Tsunamis can be highly destructive if they strike land

◀ LAVA

Lava is magma that has reached the surface. It will eventually cool and solidify to form a volcanic igneous rock such as basalt, andesite, or rhyolite. Lava can be thin, or thick and viscous. This river of molten hot lava flowing from Mount Etna is relatively thin, allowing gases to escape and the lava to flow longer distances. Thin lava will often form gently sloping shield volcanoes.

▶ TSUNAMI

Earthquakes and volcanic activity underwater can generate giant ocean waves called tsunamis. The Sumatra-Andaman earthquake in 2004 generated powerful tsunamis that devastated the coasts of Indonesia, Thailand, Sri Lanka, and India. Waves caused by the earthquake traveled as far as Struisbaai, South Africa, some 5,300 miles (8,500 km) from the epicenter.

▶ LAVA BOMB

Lava bombs are chunks of molten lava ejected from a volcano during an eruption. They can vary from the size of a golf ball to more than 17 ft (5 m) across. The 1992 eruption of Mount Spurr in Alaska saw lava bombs 3.5 ft (1 m) in size ejected up to 2 miles (3 km) from the volcano.

EXPLOSIVE ERUPTION ▼

When magma is thick and viscous, gases find it hard to escape and pressure can build. In addition, the surface opening of a volcano may be plugged with previously erupted lava. Eruptions in these situations can often be explosive, sending vast amounts of lava, rock, and ash high into the atmosphere.

SANTORINI ▼

Sometime during the period 1600–1650 BCE, a gigantic eruption occurred on the Greek island of Santorini (also known as Thera). The eruption emptied the volcano's magma chamber, which collapsed, forming a giant crater called a caldera, which flooded with water. Santorini is still the site of volcanic activity and the volcano last erupted in 1950.

Anak Krakatau has grown from the ocean floor to a height of 1,000 ft (300 m) since 1927

▼ MOUNT ETNA

Lying on the boundary between the African and Eurasian plates of Earth's crust, Mount Etna stands more than 11,000 ft (3,300 m) tall and is Europe's largest active volcano. It has a long history of activity, with five major eruptions in the 20th century alone.

▼ EXTINCT

Volcanoes can die out. Extinction can occur when Earth's plates move so that the volcano is no longer positioned above a magma chamber. Mount Kilimanjaro is a giant stratovolcano in Tanzania. It consists of three separate volcanic peaks, two of which (Mawenzi and Shira) are extinct, while one (Kibo) is classed as dormant.

▶ DORMANT

A dormant volcano is one that has not been active for a long period of time, but may erupt in the future. Mauna Kea is a dormant shield volcano and is the highest mountain in the Hawaiian Islands, with a height of 14,015 ft (4,205 m). It started building up from the Pacific floor around one million years ago and last erupted around 4,500 years ago.

ROCKS AND SOIL

Our planet's crust is formed of many different types of rocks. These materials are made up of chemical compounds called minerals. Some minerals are elements, such as the metals silver and copper. Others are compounds or mixtures, such as silicates containing oxygen, silicon, and other substances. Rocks are classified into three groups—igneous, metamorphic, and sedimentary. Over long periods of time, rocks alter their structure and can change from one group to another in a process called the rock cycle.

▼ ROCK CYCLE

The rock cycle shows how rocks can be transformed from one type to another. Sedimentary rock, for example, can be transformed into metamorphic rock through great heat and pressure. Heat can also transform sedimentary or metamorphic rock into igneous rock. Rocks can be worn away, creating particles that are transported and deposited as sediment. This settles and hardens to form new sedimentary rock.

Sedimentary rock under great heat and pressure forms metamorphic rock

Sediment deposited on seabed forms new sedimentary rock

Hot magma reaches the surface, forming igneous rock

Heat melts sedimentary rock, forming magma

▼ IGNEOUS ROCKS

Igneous rocks form when molten rock cools and solidifies. The texture of igneous rocks is determined by how quickly they cool. Those that form on or near the surface tend to cool rapidly, giving the rock a fine grain, such as basalt, the most common rock on the ocean floor. Those igneous rocks that form deep below the surface tend to cool more slowly and, as a result, tend to be tough with a coarse grain, such as granite (shown here).

IGNEOUS INTRUSIONS ▼

When magma cools and turns solid before it reaches the surface, it forms an igneous intrusion. Intrusions can form narrow dykes between cracks in other rocks, or large deep-seated batholiths. Under the surface called batholiths. Over millions of years, rocks above intrusions may wear away exposing the intrustions at the surface.

▼ SEDIMENTARY ROCKS

Sedimentary rocks, such as sandstone, are formed from tiny particles of rock or, in the case of limestone and chalk (shown here), the skeletons, shells, and other hard body parts of creatures. This material is transported and deposited by rivers, oceans, winds, or glaciers as a layer of sediment. Over time, the layers build up, heaping pressure on the layers below, which compact together to form solid rock.

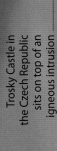

Trosky Castle in the Czech Republic sits on top of an igneous intrusion

▶ REGIONAL METAMORPHISM

Metamorphic rocks can be created over large areas, through the heat and pressure of rocks folding and bending under enormous forces, created by the movement of plates. The sedimentary rock shale, for instance, can be changed through this regional metamorphism, into slate. The slate can itself be transformed by further heat and pressure into a tough metamorphic rock called gneiss (shown here).

▲ METAMORPHIC ROCKS

Marble is a metamorphic rock. All metamorphic rocks started life as a different form of rock, before they were transformed by great heat or a combination of heat and pressure. Thermal or contact metamorphism is a process in which hot igneous rocks or magma enter an area and bake the surrounding rock. In this way, limestone can be transformed into marble (shown here) and sandstone can be changed into quartzite.

▶ SOIL

Soil is a layer of loose matter that covers large areas of land and is essential for plant growth. Soil is formed from the remains of rocks that have been broken down by weathering into tiny fragments, and mixed with decaying animal and vegetable matter, known as humus. Soil contains moisture, air, and mineral-rich nutrients taken up into plants by their roots. Soils vary greatly in composition—from thick, sticky clays to loose, dry sandy soils.

▲ ON THE SURFACE

Rivers carry vast amounts of sediment. The Amazon carries and discharges more than 1.3 million tons of sediment into the Atlantic Ocean every day. Deposition and compaction of sediment takes place close to Earth's surface. This is why around 75 percent of the rocks visible on the surface are sedimentary rocks. However, only five percent of Earth's crust is made of sedimentary rocks.

WEATHERING AND EROSION

Rock formations are continually under attack from water, wind, ice, chemical reactions, and changes in temperature. Weathering is the gradual breaking down of exposed rock. It can be caused by chemical changes or physically, when rock shatters or is broken down into smaller fragments. Erosion is the removal of weathered material from its original location. Common agents of erosion are water, wind, and ice.

◀ PHYSICAL WEATHERING

Changes in temperature cause rocks to expand when heated and contract when cold. These changes cause most physical weathering. Freeze-thaw weathering occurs when water seeps into cracks, freezes, and expands, breaking rocks apart. Salt weathering occurs when evaporating water leaves salt behind in rock holes and cracks. This salt expands when heated, pushing the rocks apart.

Holes caused by salt weathering from sea spray

▶ BIOLOGICAL WEATHERING

Living things can weather rocks. Plant roots growing between cracks widen rock fissures and split rocks apart. Some creatures, such as limpets, scrape away grains of rock surfaces or burrow into rock. Other living things, such as lichens and bacteria, secrete chemicals that can dissolve rock.

Roots of a Jeffrey pine enlarge crack in granite rock

▼ GLACIATION

Glaciers can have a dramatic impact on the landscape. They gouge, grind, and scrape out the rock as they move past, creating highland features such as jagged peaks and sharp ridges, and producing wide U-shaped valleys. When such valleys extend to the coast and are flooded with water, they are called fjords.

▲ KARST

When certain rocks, such as marble, dolomite, gypsum, and limestone, are eroded by chemical reactions with rainwater, they form Karst landscapes. Rain combines with carbon dioxide in the air to form a weak carbonic acid. Over time, this can dissolve away rock, creating large forests of rock pinnacles, or infiltrate joints in limestone formations to create caves.

The U-shaped Romsdal Valley in Norway

▶ WIND EROSION

Winds pick up large amounts of sand and other gritty particles, and blast rock surfaces. This can erode and cut grooves through softer layers of rock and sometimes round and polish harder rock. The dramatic arch of the Sipapu Bridge in Utah was originally formed by water erosion, but has been shaped subsequently by wind erosion.

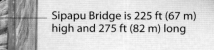

Sipapu Bridge is 225 ft (67 m) high and 275 ft (82 m) long

This meandering loop is Horseshoe Bend on the Colorado River

▶ MOVING WATER

A river's waters erode and transport vast quantities of material as sediment. Along their length, rivers cut into the surrounding land, eroding the river banks and beds, forcing water into cracks and breaking loose rock into smaller particles. When a river flows in a bend, the water current is fastest on the outside and erodes the outer bank more than the inner.

▼ COASTAL EROSION

Ocean waves erode by pounding the coastal rock with stones, sand, and other particles, which act as a powerful abrasive on the rock surface. In addition, seawater, which is mildly acidic, can dissolve limestone and chalk. Coastlines may be formed of rocks of different hardnesses and these will erode at different rates. Soft rock forming these cliffs in Chesapeake Bay in Maryland has been eroded rapidly, leaving abandoned houses teetering on the cliff edge.

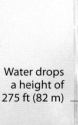

Water drops a height of 275 ft (82 m)

▲ WATERFALLS

The Iguaçu Falls in South America consists of 275 separate waterfalls called cataracts over a stretch of the Iguaçu River. Waterfalls often form when different hardnesses of rock span a river bed. The water erodes softer layers creating a steep ledge, over which the water flows. Over longer periods of time, the waterfall erodes the harder rock as well, so the falls retreat upriver.

FOSSILS AND STRATA

Rock formations provide varying branches of geology (the study of rocks) and paleontology (the study of prehistoric life) with clues to the distant past. Fossils can lie buried for tens or hundreds of millions of years until rock movement or erosion reveal them. Earth has a 4.6-billion-year-long history. To deal with the enormous time spans involved in rock and fossil history, scientists use the concept of geologic time.

❶ GEOLOGIC TIME

Earth's history is divided into four major eras of geologic time—the Proterozoic, Paleozoic, Mesozoic, and Cenozoic. The Cenozoic era extends from 65 million years ago to the present day. Each era is split into periods, which are subdivided into epochs. We are currently living in the Holocene epoch, which began 10,000 years ago.

❷ LAYER ON LAYER

These rock formations in Arizona's Painted Desert show layers or strata of sedimentary rocks. Over long periods of time, sedimentary rocks form layers on top of each other. In an undisturbed rock formation, the oldest layers are at the bottom. Geologists can investigate strata to build a picture of the geologic history of an area.

❶

Eras	Late Proterozoic			Paleozoic							Mesozoic			Cenozoic		
Periods	Tonian	Cryogenian	Ediacaran	Cambrian	Ordovician	Silurian	Devonian	Carboniferous	Permian	Triassic	Jurassic	Cretaceous	Paleogene	Neogene	Quaternary

850   630   542   488   443   416   359   299   251   200   146   65   23   1.8   0

1,000 million years ago

❷

❸

❹

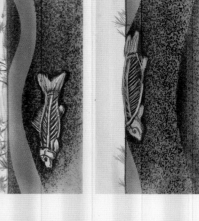

❺

Fish dies

Remains covered by silt

Soft body parts replaced by silt and skeletal remains replaced by minerals

Fossilized remains become exposed at surface

❸ FAULTING AND BENDING

Many rock formations do not remain undisturbed for millions of years. Movements in the crust can cause rock strata to snap and move. Less violent pressure and heat can deform rocks over long periods of time. This can bend and fold rock strata. This image shows an anticline fold—an upward-pointing fold with its oldest rocks farthest from the surface.

❹ FOSSILS

Fossils are any physical evidence of former prehistoric life. This means that ancient feces that have been preserved or a dinosaur footprint are fossils, as well as complete skeletons of dinosaurs or the outer shell of a prehistoric marine animal. Fossils form in a number of different ways, including insects being trapped in sticky resin from trees that hardens to form amber.

Dragonfly fossil from the Mesozoic era (251–65 million years ago)

More than 65,000 fossils have been recovered from the Burgess Shale site

Models of mammoths caught in La Brea Tar Pits

❺ FOSSILIZATION

This diagram shows how a prehistoric fish can become a fossil. A dead fish's soft body parts rot away, but its bones and other hard body parts remain and can be infiltrated by minerals. These harden as layer upon layer of sediment covers the remains. Erosion and movements in the crust can expose the fossil.

❻ PRESERVING IN TAR

The remains of some prehistoric creatures were well preserved when they fell into pits of thick tar or asphalt. The La Brea Tar Pits in Los Angeles, California, are world-famous for preserving thousands of fossils that are up to 40,000 years old. These fossils include the remains of mammoths and saber-toothed tigers.

❼ FOSSIL FINDS

Many sites have become renowned for their rich haul of discovered fossils. Canada's Burgess Shale formation was discovered in 1909. Dating back to the Middle Cambrian period 520–512 million years ago, the area was part of an ocean where frequent mudslides preserved the remains of marine creatures.

❽ FOSSIL REMAINS

Scientists interpret fossils to build a picture of prehistoric life, climate, and the geography of regions millions of years ago. Certain species that evolved rapidly and were distributed widely around the planet are called index fossils. Rocks containing these fossils date the rock to that time.

WATER

Water is essential to life. It makes up more than 50 percent of the weight of all living things, and few organisms can survive for long without it. There is an estimated 350 million cubic miles (1.45 billion cubic km) of water on the planet existing in solid, liquid, and gaseous states. The total amount of water found on Earth never changes, but it moves from place to place and state to state in a continuous process called the water cycle.

▲ ICE CAPS

Less than three percent of the world's water is freshwater. Most of this is locked up as solid ice in glaciers and in the giant ice sheets that cover parts of the Arctic and much of the continent of Antarctica. The Antarctic ice sheet is enormous. It has an area of almost 5.5 million square miles (14 million square km) and extends down in places to depths of 8,200 ft (2,500 m).

◀ SEAS AND OCEANS

Seas and oceans cover almost three-quarters of the planet's surface. Together, they hold more than 97 percent of all the water on Earth. Seawater is saline (salty), typically three percent salt and 0.6 percent other elements, such as potassium, fluoride, and calcium. The planet's oceans are all interconnected and water is pushed around by ocean currents.

Highland area

Mature river winds across landscape

River mouth

Water empties into sea

Water vapor forms clouds

Water evaporates from seas and oceans

Precipitation falls to ground

Water transpires from plants

Water flows in rivers to seas and oceans

◀ RIVERS

Most rivers are fed by smaller rivers and streams called tributaries as well as by falling rain and melting ice from highland regions. They slow in speed and tend to widen and meander in bends as they reach lowland areas. Eventually, they flow into lakes, fan out into wetlands and deltas, or empty into the sea.

▲ THE WATER CYCLE

The Sun powers the water cycle. It evaporates liquid water into water vapor in the atmosphere. Water vapor is also sent into the atmosphere by plants through transpiration. Winds transport the water vapor around before it falls as rain, snow, hail, and other forms of precipitation.

◀ CLOUD FORMATION

Clouds form when warm air containing water vapor rises and cools, and the vapor condenses to form millions of small water droplets. As these droplets collide, they form larger drops, which become too heavy for the air to support. These droplets may fall to Earth as rain or, if it is cold enough, as snow, sleet, or hail.

▶ TOO LITTLE WATER

Droughts are long periods with no rain or far lower than average rainfall. As a result, an imbalance occurs in water supplies, with reservoirs and wells drying up and crops failing. Droughts cause soils to harden, crack into lumps, and crumble into dust that may be blown away. This great loss of soil can leave regions in crisis even when rain returns.

▶ WETLANDS

Areas of land that are saturated with water, where still or slow-moving water is present, are called wetlands. This water forms marshes, lagoons, swamps, and bogs. Wetlands, such as the Okavango Delta in Botswana, form very rich habitats. Fed by annual floodwaters, the Okavango can swell to cover an area of up to 6,000 square miles (15,000 square km).

▼ TOO MUCH WATER

Many floods occur regularly and predictably. Some, such as the flooding of the Nile River in Egypt, can be very useful since the floodwaters deposit rich, fertile sediment that is good for crop growing, while much of the water is stored for irrigation. Unexpected flooding, however, can be devastating. It can destroy towns, crops, and animal habitats.

The Okavango is the world's largest inland delta

Floodwaters swamp the town of Fenton, Missouri

WEATHER

Air in the atmosphere is always on the move, carrying clouds, rain, and snow around the globe. The weather is generated by air currents that circulate through the atmosphere, driven by the heat of the Sun. These currents carry areas of cold and warmer air at different pressures. Weather describes the day-to-day state of the atmosphere over an area. A region's climate is the general weather conditions it experiences over a long period of time.

❶ Snow Water droplets can freeze into ice crystals in clouds. These collide with each other, sticking together to form snowflakes. Most melt on the way to the ground and fall as rain. If the air close to the ground is cold enough, some will fall as snow. Snowfall can be light or severe. Thompson Pass in Alaska once received 63 in (160 cm) of snowfall in a day.

❷ Humidity This is a measure of the amount of moisture (water vapor) in the air. In general, the hotter the air, the more moisture it can hold. Humid conditions mean that sweat from bodies cannot evaporate as quickly. This is why a very humid day can feel hotter and more uncomfortable than a dry day with the same temperature.

❸ Hailstones These are pieces of ice that form inside storm clouds. Hail forms when ice crystals descend through a cloud, picking up a layer of moisture on their outer surface. Strong air currents sweep them back up through the cloud, where this moisture freezes to add a new layer of ice. Successive cycles create large hailstones containing many layers, which then fall to Earth. A hailstone recovered in Aurora, Nebraska, in 2003 had a diameter of 7 in (18 cm) and weighed 1.5 lb (680 g).

❹ Fog When water-vapor clouds form at or near ground level and reduce visibility at ground level to less than 0.6 miles (1 km), they are known as fog. This can be a safety issue for road traffic, aircraft, and shipping. In areas with significant air pollution from coal burning and vehicle emissions, smoke can react with fog to form photochemical smog containing substances that are harmful to health.

Golf ball–sized hailstone that fell in Texas

5 Wind Differences in temperature and air pressure cause the streams of moving air that we feel as wind. Different parts of the world receive different amounts of the Sun's heat. Colder air from the poles tends to sink and move toward the equator close to the surface of the Earth. Warm air from the equator rises and moves toward the poles high in the atmosphere because it is less dense.

Updrafts (upward-rising air currents) in storm clouds can travel at more than 80 mph (130 km/h)

Air surrounding lightning can reach temperatures of 36,000°F (20,000°C).

Weather maps show the positions of the fronts of warm and cold air masses as red and blue lines

6 Lightning When a huge electrical discharge is released from the atmosphere during a storm, we see a flash of lightning. Colliding ice crystals in storm clouds build up positive and negative electrical charges. As these charged particles move to equal themselves out, they can cause a giant spark of lightning. Thunder is created by hot air around lightning expanding rapidly and violently.

7 Storms Cumulonimbus storm clouds have their base close to the ground but extend upward into the atmosphere more than 7.5 miles (12 km). Storms are disturbances in the atmosphere often caused where warm and cold air masses meet. Winds build in speed and moisture falls as rain, snow, or hail. A 2005 storm over the city of Mumbai, India, brought 37 in (944 mm) of rainfall in a single day.

8 Hurricanes Also known as typhoons or cyclones, hurricanes develop over tropical oceans. They are giant storms, often measuring more than 400 miles (600 km) in diameter with winds circulating at speeds up to 200 mph (300 km/h) around a relatively calm center called the eye. Hurricanes can cause immense destruction. Hurricane Felix struck Central America in 2007, causing more than 130 deaths.

9 Weather map Meteorologists, or weather experts, map existing weather patterns and forecast future weather. Weather balloons, weather stations dotted around the globe, and satellites send data to powerful computers to track conditions in the atmosphere, the strengths of winds, and the buildup of storms. However, forecasts can often be inaccurate since weather conditions can change suddenly.

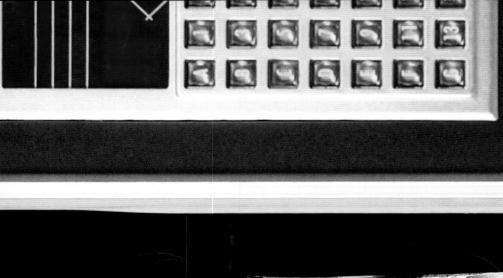

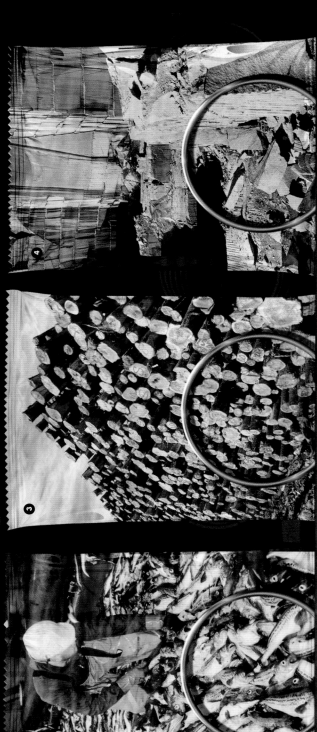

NATURAL RESOURCES

The Earth provides humankind with a wide range of resources. A river, for example, provides not only drinking and cleaning water, but also potentially rich food sources and a transportation system for boats and shipping. Similarly, forests offer shelter, food, fuel, medicine, and valuable raw materials for construction, paper, and other industries. However, these resources have to be used carefully. Overuse can deplete stocks and reduce the supply of a resource, while careless use of methods and chemicals can damage the environment or even destroy a resource completely.

❶ Farming About 10,000 years ago, humans learned how to cultivate wild plants and rear animals to supply food. Today, farming is an enormous industry. In 2009 alone, 682 million tons of wheat was produced worldwide. However, farming requires a huge amount of land, which first needs to be cleared of forests, grasslands, and other native environments.

❺ Mining and ores Mining can be performed deep underground or in an open pit on the surface. Mines are dug to obtain coal, gemstones, metals, and minerals, such as feldspar and potash. Many of the most useful metals on the planet, including iron, aluminum, and copper, are found in the Earth's crust in rocky ores. These have to be processed to extract the metal from the ore.

❷ Riches from the sea Commercial fishing employs more than 35 million people worldwide. Its catch, ranging from tiny crustaceans to tuna weighing more than 440 lb (200 kg), provides foods that are rich in protein and nutrients. Overfishing in certain areas, however, has caused a drastic reduction in fish stocks. This has led to many governments introducing limits on how many fish can be caught.

❻ Fossil fuels Natural gas, coal, and oil are all fossil fuels. These are the remains of dead organisms that have changed into energy sources. Power plants that burn fossil fuels produce 60 percent of our electricity. However, fossil fuels are a limited resource and humans are having to go to more extreme lengths to find new sources, searching deep beneath the oceans or under the polar ice caps.

❸ Forestry Millions of tons of wood is cut down every year for use in the timber industry. In addition to timber, the world's forests are rich in other resources, including medicinal plants and foods. In industry today, a range of substances is extracted from wood. These include cellulose used in textiles and paints, and other chemicals used as fragrances and food flavorings.

❼ Hydroelectric power This is a form of renewable energy that has been used to power water mills and waterwheels for centuries. Today, it is used to turn turbines to produce electricity. Around one-fifth of the world's electricity is produced this way. Hydroelectric dams, such as the Hoover Dam, create huge lakes behind them. These lakes can flood entire towns or areas of environmental importance.

❹ Rocky raw materials Many rocks and minerals are used in a whole range of industries, from cosmetics (clays) to food preparation (rock salt). Limestone and granite are quarried as building stone or, in the case of limestone, crushed to make types of cement. Among sand's many uses is the manufacture of glass, while clay and shale are used to make bricks and ceramics.

❽ Sun, wind, and sea Renewable energies also include wind power, solar power, and wave and tidal power. Wind turbines, for example, generate turning movements to power electricity-generating turbines. Around two percent of the world's electricity is generated by wind power, but in some countries, the amount is far higher—20 percent in Denmark and 14 percent in Spain.

HUMAN IMPACT

In 1900, the estimated world human population was around 1.6 billion. Just 100 years later, it had increased more than four times, passing 6.9 billion in 2010. This phenomenal boom in the number of people has put the planet under increasing strain as a rapidly growing human population demands food, clothing, land, shelter, electricity, and other resources. Poor management of resources and the generation of large amounts of air, water, and land pollution threaten the environment and wildlife.

▼ AIR POLLUTION

Every day, millions of tons of pollutants, including carbon monoxide, carbon dioxide, sulfur dioxide, and tiny solid particles, are pumped into the atmosphere. The main culprits are motor vehicles, industrial emissions, and power plants that burn fossil fuels, such as coal and oil.

Tree damaged by acid rain in North Carolina

▶ ACID RAIN

Sulfur dioxide, nitrogen oxides, and other pollutants from factories, coal-fired power plants, and vehicle emissions can enter the atmosphere and mix with water vapor. Blown some distance from where they were released, these pollutants fall back to Earth in acid rain. This can kill trees, dissolve and wash away nutrients and minerals in the soil, destroy life in lakes and rivers, and erode stone.

Polluted water runs into wetlands, destroying habitats and life

WATER POLLUTION ▲

Water is one of the most fundamental resources for life and it is abundant over the planet as a whole. Yet more than 800 million people lack a clean water supply and have to drink unsafe water that carries deadly diseases. Human and animal sewage flushed into streams and rivers without being treated damages clean water supplies. Additional pollution of seas, oceans, lakes, and rivers comes from industry, chemical, and oil spills, and rain washing pesticides and fertilizers off farmland into rivers and streams.

▶ DEFORESTATION

At least a third of the world's rainforests have disappeared in the past century. The trees have been cut for timber or fuel, or the land cleared for farmland or settlements.

This deforestation has destroyed incredibly rich habitats, threatening many plant and animal species with extinction and reducing the planet's ability to absorb carbon dioxide through the leaves of trees.

A pile of logs stacked up in a forest clearing

▶ DESERTIFICATION

Deforestation, soil erosion, overgrazing, and climate change are all factors in the increasing amount of land turning into dust bowls unsuitable for cultivation. Desertification is a widespread problem in Africa, Central and Latin America, Central Asia, and China. Every year, around 30 million acres (12 million hectares) of land, an area larger than the country of Portugal, become too desertlike to grow crops.

▶ CLIMATE CHANGE

Earth's atmosphere has always contained carbon dioxide, methane, and other "greenhouse" gases that trap heat and warm the planet's surface. In recent years, however, it is believed that an increase in greenhouse gases in the atmosphere, caused by human activity, has been leading to a general increase in world temperatures. Climate change could lead to rising sea levels, melting ice caps, changing weather patterns, and the extinction of many species.

Coral bleaching caused by rising sea temperatures

▶ WASTE DISPOSAL

Vast amounts of waste are generated every day. In 2008, the United States alone produced more than 250 million tons of waste. Much of this waste is burned in incinerators, releasing additional air pollution, buried in landfill sites, or left to decay in open mounds. Water runoff from landfills can carry poisonous substances that pollute water sources above and below ground.

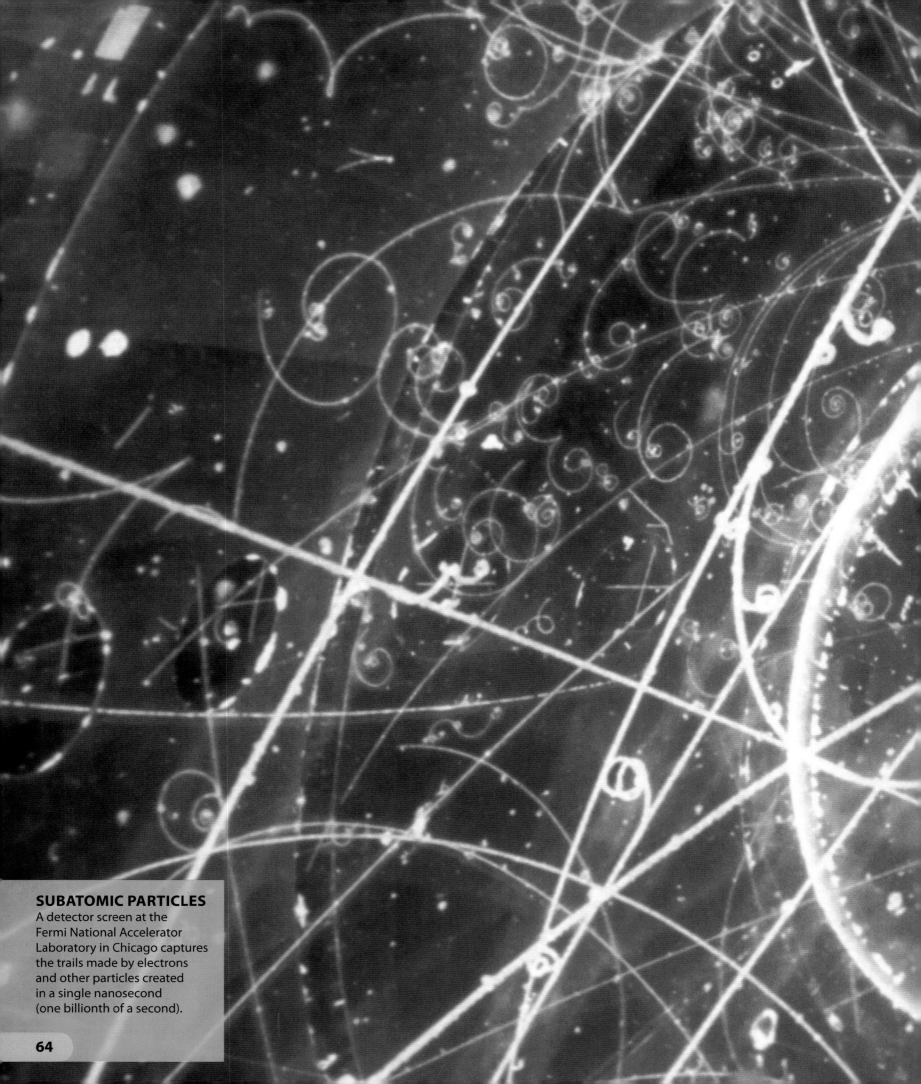

SUBATOMIC PARTICLES
A detector screen at the
Fermi National Accelerator
Laboratory in Chicago captures
the trails made by electrons
and other particles created
in a single nanosecond
(one billionth of a second).

Matter and materials

BUILDING BLOCKS

All matter, from our bodies and the air we breathe to the ink, paper, and cover that make up this book, consists of atoms. An atom, from the ancient Greek word for indivisible, is the smallest amount of a substance that can exist and retain the properties of that substance. Each different type of atom is called an element, and more than 100 exist. A typical atom has a radius of just one tenth of a billionth of a meter.

Electron orbit in outer shell

◀ ATOMIC STRUCTURE

An atom is mostly empty space. At its center is a nucleus made up of particles with a positive electric charge called protons and electrically neutral neutrons. Orbiting the nucleus are electrons—atomic particles with a negative electrical charge. The pull between the charges of the electrons and protons causes the electrons to orbit the nucleus, arranged in different layers, or shells. An atom of nitrogen (see left) has a nucleus with seven protons and seven neutrons. Seven electrons orbit the nucleus in two shells.

ISOTOPES ▶

In some cases, atoms of the same element can have different numbers of neutrons in their nucleus. Each of the possible versions of an element is known as an isotope. In its most common form, hydrogen is the one element with no neutrons in its nucleus. Two isotopes of hydrogen exist, however—deuterium, with one neutron, and tritium, with two. The most common form of carbon has six neutrons but the isotope carbon-14 has eight neutrons.

Carbon-14 has equal numbers of protons and electrons (six), but eight neutrons

MOLECULES—OXYGEN ▶

It is relatively rare for atoms to be found on their own. They tend to combine with other atoms, either of the same type or of other elements to form a molecule. A molecule has chemical bonds between its atoms and can be shown by a chemical formula—a combination of letters and numbers that show the types of atoms and their proportion in a molecule. Oxygen has the chemical symbol O, but oxygen molecules are diatomic—they contain two atoms. So an oxygen molecule's chemical formula is O_2.

Oxygen atom chemically bonded to another to form oxygen molecule

MOLECULES—SULFUR ▶

Eight sulfur atoms bond in a ring to form a molecule of this yellow solid. Sulfur reacts with many other elements to form a wide range of compounds (combination of two or more elements). It reacts with all metals except gold and platinum. There are around 30 different isotopes of sulfur, only a few of which are stable and do not react easily with other substances. Sulfur is used in the process of making substances such as fertilizers, gunpowder, and many medical drugs.

Sulfur (S_8) molecule, made of eight sulfur atoms

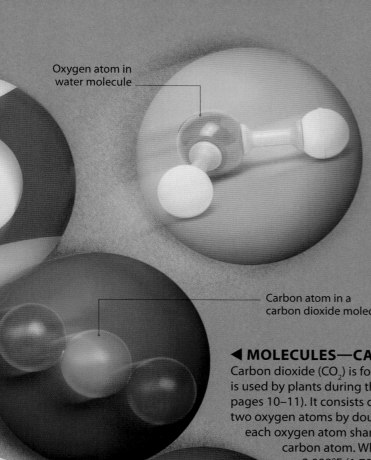

Oxygen atom in
water molecule

◀ **MOLECULES—WATER**

Ancient philosophers thought of water
as one of the four or five fundamental
elements that made up the Universe.
Today, we know that water is itself
composed of two different elements.
Two atoms of hydrogen combine with
one atom of oxygen to form a molecule
of water (H_2O). Water can be split back
into its constituent elements by the
process of electrolysis.

Carbon atom in a
carbon dioxide molecule

◀ **MOLECULES—CARBON DIOXIDE**

Carbon dioxide (CO_2) is found in the atmosphere as a gas and
is used by plants during the process of photosynthesis (see
pages 10–11). It consists of one carbon atom that is joined to
two oxygen atoms by double covalent bonds. This means that
each oxygen atom shares two pairs of electrons with the
carbon atom. When heated to temperatures above
3,000°F (1,700°C), it splits into oxygen and
carbon monoxide (CO).

◀ **MOLECULES—METHANE**

Methane has the chemical formula CH_4 and has the molecular
structure of four hydrogen atoms all joined to one carbon
atom. Methane is colorless and odorless and is a major
constituent of natural gas found in reserves on Earth. It is also
common in the atmospheres of the planets Neptune, Jupiter,
Uranus, and Saturn. Recent increases in the levels of methane gas
in the atmosphere may be a significant cause of global warming.

▼ **SPLITTING ATOMS**

Atomic science has developed techniques for nuclear
fission—splitting the nuclei of certain atoms to generate
enormous amounts of power. This can be used for destructive
purposes in bombs or to generate superheated steam in
nuclear power plants to drive turbines to generate electricity.
In a nuclear power plant, neutrons bombard uranium-235
atoms, splitting nuclei and releasing
more neutrons. These start a
chain reaction by splitting
more nuclei and releasing
yet more neutrons.

Propane's chemical
formula is C_3H_8

◀ **MOLECULES—PROPANE**

Substances whose molecules
consist only of hydrogen and carbon
atoms are known as hydrocarbons.
Methane and propane are hydrocarbons.
Propane is a colorless gas that can be readily
turned into a liquid for transportation and
storage. It is separated in large quantities from
natural gas, crude oil, and oil-refinery gases. It is
used as a fuel and is also an important raw
material in the chemical industry.

A detonated atomic
bomb produces
a giant mushroom
cloud in the
atmosphere

THE PERIODIC TABLE

Elements consist of one type of atom. They are pure substances and they cannot be broken down into simpler substances. For example, water contains both hydrogen (H) and oxygen (O) atoms, so it is not an element, but hydrogen is. Each element has a different atomic number—the number of protons in the atom's nucleus. Ninety of the first 92 elements by atomic number occur naturally. Hydrogen is the lightest and most abundant element in the Universe and it has the atomic number 1.

❶ PERIODIC TABLE
Based on the work of Russian scientist, Dmitri Mendeleev (1834–1907), the periodic table is a list of all elements. The elements are arranged in columns called groups and horizontal rows called periods. Each element to the right of another in the same period has an extra electron in its atoms. Elements in the same group tend to share similar chemical properties.

❷ ALKALI METALS
The first group in the periodic table includes lithium, potassium, and the most abundant alkali metal, sodium. These metals all react with water, forming alkaline solutions as a result. In the case of cesium (Cs) and rubidium (Rb), their reaction with water is an explosive one. Alkali metals are soft, white-colored, and rarely found in their pure form in nature.

Lithium (Li)

Sodium (Na)

Potassium (K)

Nickel (Ni)

Iron (Fe)

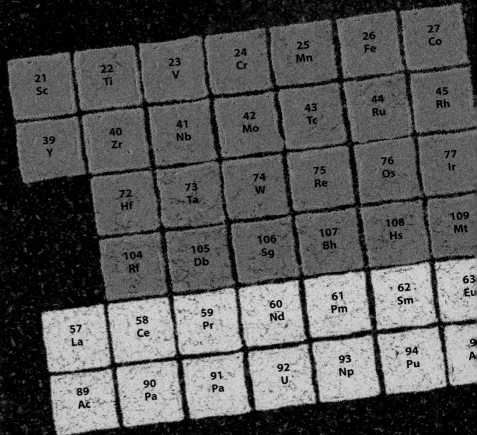

1 H									
3 Li	4 Be								
11 Na	12 Mg								
19 K	20 Ca	21 Sc	22 Ti	23 V	24 Cr	25 Mn	26 Fe	27 Co
37 Rb	38 Sr	39 Y	40 Zr	41 Nb	42 Mo	43 Tc	44 Ru	45 Rh
55 Cs	56 Ba	72 Hf	73 Ta	74 W	75 Re	76 Os	77 Ir
87 Fr	88 Ra	104 Rf	105 Db	106 Sg	107 Bh	108 Hs	109 Mt

57 La	58 Ce	59 Pr	60 Nd	61 Pm	62 Sm	63 Eu
89 Ac	90 Pa	91 Pa	92 U	93 Np	94 Pu	

Calcium (Ca)

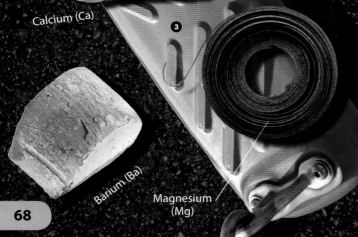

Barium (Ba)

Magnesium (Mg)

❸ ALKALINE-EARTH METALS
Calcium, magnesium, barium, and radium (Ra) are all alkaline-earth metals, found in compounds in Earth's crust. Beryllium (Be), for example, is found in gemstones, such as beryl and emeralds. Alkaline-earth metals react with water, though less intensely than alkali metals, and with oxygen. Magnesium burns a bright white in air and is used for flares and fireworks.

❹ TRANSITION METALS

This large group of elements includes some of the most common metals, such as copper and chromium. They include elements that can create a magnetic field, such as nickel and iron, and the most dense naturally occurring element, osmium (Os). While mercury (Hg) is a liquid at room temperature, transition metals tend to have high melting points. They also tend to be hard and their outer electrons are capable of flowing, making them good conductors of heat and electricity.

Copper (Cu)

Chromium (Cr)

❻ NOBLE GASES

These gases are colorless and odorless and largely unreactive, but that does not mean they lack useful applications. Helium is the second lightest gas after hydrogen, but does not burn, making it safe for use in deep-sea diving and airships. With the exception of helium, all noble gases emit light if electricity is passed through them and thus are used for lighting.

Helium (He)

Argon (Ar)

Neon (Ne)

❼ NONMETALS

Nonmetals include common gases in the atmosphere, such as nitrogen and oxygen, as well as sulfur (S) and carbon. Nonmetals tend to be poor conductors of heat and electricity and are brittle when solid. Halogens, such as chlorine (Cl), are a type of nonmetal that form salts with other elements.

Oxygen (O)

Carbon (C)

Nitrogen (N)

												2 He
			5 B	6 C	7 N	8 O	9 F	10 Ne
			13 Al	14 Si	15 P	16 S	17 Ci	18 Ar
28 Ni	29 Cu	30 Zn	31 Ga	32 Ge	33 As	34 Se	35 Br	36 Kr
46 Pd	47 Ag	48 Cd	49 In	50 Sn	51 Sb	52 Te	53 I	54 Xe
78 Pt	79 Au	80 Hg	81 Ti	82 Pb	83 Bi	84 Po	85 At	86 Rn

64 Gd	65 Tb	66 Dy	67 Ho	68 Er	69 Tm	70 Yb	71 Lu
96 Cm	97 Bk	98 Cf	99 Es	100 Fm	101 Md	102 No	103 Lr

❺ POOR AND SEMIMETALS

Lead, tin, aluminum, and bismuth (Bi) are all poor metals. These are softer and have lower melting points than transition metals. Most poor metals are at their most useful when mixed with another metal in an alloy such as bronze (an alloy of copper and tin). Semimetals, such as arsenic (As), antimony (Sb), boron (B), and silicon (Si), possess some, but not all, properties of metals.

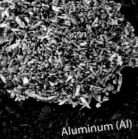
Aluminum (Al)

Lead (Pb)

Tin (Sn)

STATES OF MATTER

Matter exists in different physical states—solid, liquid, water, and plasma. A substance or element can change its physical state, but still retains the same chemical makeup. Oxygen, for example, is a gas at room temperature, but can be cooled to form a liquid and it still remains oxygen. Water is unusual since it is found on Earth in three states—solid ice, liquid water, and gaseous water vapor. Solids usually change state into liquids, but frozen carbon dioxide, known as dry ice, can change state directly into a gas. This process is called sublimation.

❶ EVAPORATION

Evaporation is the process by which a liquid changes its state into a gas. The opposite change of state from gas to liquid is called condensation. Evaporation occurs when some molecules in a liquid have enough energy to escape the liquid's surface as a gas. Liquid water on pavement or in wet clothes evaporates into the atmosphere as water vapor. Liquids evaporate more quickly as they heat up, such as when water is boiled in a kettle.

❷ LIQUIDS

Molecules in a liquid are very close, but can slip over each other to change position. Liquids have a definite volume, but no definite shape. They can be pushed along a pipe, but they cannot be compressed to occupy less space. Liquids can flow and take on the shape of the container they occupy. Viscosity is a measure of how easily a liquid flows. Liquids with a high viscosity, such as thick syrups and shampoos, flow less freely.

Boiled in a kettle, water changes state and rises as steam

Fruit juice has low viscosity and flows freely

❸ SOLIDS

Atoms and molecules are packed tightly together in solids, sometimes in a regular lattice. The particles in a solid still move but their movement is a small vibration. As a result, solids have a definite shape, from a long, thin piece of copper wire to a round china saucer or square-shaped piece of toast. Solids also have a defined volume and occupy a definite space.

❹ GASES

The molecules in a gas are far apart and can move freely and rapidly. As a result, gases can expand to fill a container and have a low density. Gases do not have a fixed shape or volume so they can be compressed, reducing the space between their particles. Most gases are invisible. Steam rising from a hot cup of coffee is only visible as it starts to condense and forms a mist of water droplets.

❺ MELTING

Matter melts when it changes state from a solid to a liquid. Increased temperature can cause the particles in a solid to vibrate more and more quickly. Eventually, they are able to slip over each other and form a liquid. The temperature this happens at is called the melting point. The metal tungsten has an extremely high melting point of approximately 6,190°F (3,420°C).

❻ FREEZING

Freezing occurs when substances change from liquids to solids, such as solid ice forming from liquid water or liquid wax running down a candle and hardening into solid wax. Different substances have different freezing points, the point below which they will turn from a liquid to a solid. Pure water has a freezing point of 32°F (0°C), while mercury's freezing point is -37.8°F (-38.8°C).

❼ PLASMA

Plasma is the fourth state of matter. It is found throughout the Universe, but rarely on Earth. It is a gaslike state caused when either radiation or extremely high temperatures strip electrons away from atoms. This creates a gaseous cloud of positive ions and negative electrons. Plasma conducts heat and electricity extremely well and is found around stars like the Sun and in the natural light displays in the sky called auroras.

Aurora Borealis lights shine in the night sky of the northern hemisphere

Butter has a low melting point of between 72°F (22°C) and 113°F (45°C), depending on its fat and water content

Solid ice cubes melt slowly in water

PROPERTIES OF MATTER

All materials and substances have a wide range of different characteristics called properties. These describe attributes ranging from appearance—color, luster (whether something is shiny or not), and smell—to chemical properties, such as a substance's ability to dissolve in liquids, its acidity, and whether it will combust or not. This information is used in industry and by scientists and engineers to select the right material or substance for a particular task.

▶ HARDNESS

The property of hardness is a measure of how easy or difficult it is to permanently scratch or shape a substance. Different measurements of hardness are made. One common method is the Mohs scale, which places 10 minerals on a scale of softness and hardness and measures how well one substance will resist scratching by another.

Talc is rated 1—the softest mineral on the Mohs scale

Diamond can scratch talc, corundum, and all other minerals on the Mohs scale

Corundum is a very hard mineral and can scratch anything except for diamond

▼ MASS AND DENSITY

Density is how heavy something is for its size. It is calculated by dividing the material's mass by its volume. Dense materials, such as lead and brass, are used for weights, while materials with low density, such as wood, float in water. These air-filled plastic foam pellets have very low density and are used to protect electronic goods and other delicate items.

Air-filled foam pellets have less than a tenth the density of water

▼ FLEXIBILITY AND ELASTICITY

Some materials are more flexible and able to bend more than others. Elasticity is the ability of a material to absorb force and bend or stretch in different directions, before returning to its original position. Some materials have an elastic limit. If stretched beyond it, they do not return to their original size and shape.

A rubber band is both flexible and elastic; it can be bent and stretched before returning to its original shape

▼ CONDUCTING ELECTRICITY

Materials with good electrical conductivity allow an electric current to flow through them easily. Metals are all excellent conductors. Copper, especially, is used in electrical wiring. Glass, ceramics, and plastics are poor conductors of electricity. They are used as insulators, preventing electricity from flowing where it is not wanted, for example by isolating a pylon carrying high-voltage electricity from a power plant to homes.

Ceramic disks insulate pylons from the electricity-carrying cables

This red-hot iron bar would have to be handled with thick gloves

▲ THERMAL CONDUCTIVITY

Heat moves through materials at differing rates depending on the material and how thermally conductive it is. If a metal spoon is placed in a cup of water that is heated from below, the spoon handle quickly becomes hot. This is because both water and most metals are excellent conductors of heat. Materials that are poor thermal conductors, like glass and plastics, are usually excellent insulators and resist the flow of heat through them.

▶ SOLUBILITY

Some materials are soluble and can dissolve in water or other liquids to form a solution. Water is sometimes called the universal solvent since many substances can dissolve in it. A carbonated soft drink consists of soluble sweeteners, flavorings, and carbon dioxide to give the drink its fizz, all dissolved in water.

Gold is very malleable and can be beaten into thin sheets called gold leaf

▲ PLASTICITY

Plasticity is the ability of a material to be shaped or deformed permanently. There are different forms of plasticity, including ductility, the ability of a material to be drawn into thin wires, and malleability, the ability of a material to be beaten into thin sheets.

▼ FLAMMABILITY

Flammability describes how easily a material ignites (catches fire) and then combusts (burns). Some materials are highly flammable and burn readily, producing heat. Nearly all motor vehicles rely on liquid gasoline's flammability, burning it inside engine cylinders to drive pistons. A material that does not burn is said to be nonflammable.

CHEMICAL REACTIONS

A chemical reaction occurs when the bonds between atoms and molecules in substances are broken and then reformed into different chemical substances. The original substances are called reactants and the results of the reaction are called products. When a substance contains two or more elements, it is called a compound. Chemical reactions can be sudden, such as an explosion, or can take place over many years, such as the tarnishing of silver in contact with air.

❸ DISPLACEMENT REACTIONS

Some reactions involve one element replacing another in a compound (a substance in which two or more elements have combined chemically). The more reactive element displaces the less reactive element. Galvanizing is a method of rustproofing iron or steel objects, such as a trash can. A thin layer of zinc coats the iron or steel object. If the iron is exposed and iron oxide rust threatens, the zinc will displace the iron, forming zinc oxide.

❶ REDOX REACTIONS

These involve both oxidation and reduction reactions. Oxidation occurs when substances combine with oxygen or lose hydrogen. At the same time, other substances are undergoing a reduction reaction, losing oxygen or gaining hydrogen. Metal corrosion is a redox reaction. Corrosion causes metals to lose their shine, and their structure may break down, such as when rust eats through metal.

❷ REVERSIBLE REACTIONS

Most reactions only go one way. They are irreversible, since the reactants are used up to form new products. In a small number of reactions, however, some of the reactants remain and the reaction can reverse. Molecules of ammonia gas and hydrogen chloride gas are formed when solid ammonium chloride is heated. Some of these gases immediately react with each other to form ammonium chloride again.

❹ EXOTHERMIC REACTIONS

Reactions that give off energy to their surroundings, usually in the form of heat, are called exothermic reactions. Neutralization reactions between acids and alkalis give off energy, as do combustion reactions. These are a type of rapid oxidation reaction in which fuel combines with oxygen, generating heat and sometimes light. The burning of hydrocarbons, such as oil or coal, is a combustion reaction that provides us with the energy to power our cars and homes.

Red iron oxides (rust) form when iron reacts with water and oxygen in air

Ammonia molecule contains one nitrogen and three hydrogen atoms

❺ ENDOTHERMIC REACTIONS

During some reactions, more energy is needed to break molecular bonds than is released when new bonds are made. These reactions take in energy, usually in the form of heat, from their surroundings. This leaves the surrounding area cooler as a result. An ice pack used to treat a sprain or bruise contains water and ammonium chloride. When the pack is activated, the barrier between the two substances is broken and the substances mix and react, drawing in heat and making the pack ice-cold.

❻ RATE OF REACTION

The speed of chemical reactions can change depending on factors such as temperature, the size of the particles, or the amount of light. Most reaction rates increase if the temperature is higher, since the particles move more rapidly. Solids tend to react more quickly if they are broken up into smaller pieces since the pieces then have a greater total surface area than when they were a single piece. This fork is made of a biodegradable plastic derived from corn. It decays in just 45 days compared to the many years regular plastics can take to decay.

❼ CATALYSTS

A catalyst is a substance that is used to alter the rate of a chemical reaction. Some catalysts, known as inhibitors, slow the rate of a reaction. They are used to prevent bread from going stale or rust occurring inside iron radiators. Most catalysts speed up the rate of reaction. Platinum, palladium, and rhodium in a car's catalytic converter react with the toxic emissions from a gasoline engine to convert nitrous oxides and carbon monoxide into carbon dioxide and harmless nitrogen and oxygen.

Bunsen burner combusts methane, producing carbon dioxide and water

Day 0

Day 12

Day 33

Day 45

MIXTURES AND COMPOUNDS

Mixtures are physical combinations of substances, such as soil, muddy water, or ink. The atoms, molecules, or particles of the different substances are mingled thoroughly with each other, but have not chemically bonded to form different substances. Compounds are also made up of several different atoms. However, they are made from two or more elements that have chemically reacted with each other and are held together by chemical bonds.

❶ COMPOUNDS

The elements found in a compound are usually in fixed proportion to each other, so a beaker of water (below) contains molecules that each have two hydrogen atoms and one oxygen atom. Compounds cannot be separated by physical means. It takes a chemical reaction to break the bonds between their molecules. Compounds often possess quite different properties than their constituent elements. Sodium chloride is white, granular common salt, but it is made up of a silvery metal, sodium, and a gas, chlorine.

❸ MIXING IT UP

Solutions are uniform mixtures, in which two or more substances are mixed together evenly. The substance present in the greatest amount is known as the solvent. Other substances, called solutes, dissolve into the solvent. Air is a gaseous solution of oxygen and other gases dissolved in nitrogen. Most solutions are gases or solids dissolved in a liquid. A standard saline drip (right) contains a solution of 0.9 percent sodium chloride dissolved in sterile water. It is given to hospital patients to prevent dehydration.

❷ POLYMERS

Polymers are compounds that form long repeating chains of molecules. Some polymers exist in nature, such as hair fibers, DNA, and cellulose (shown below), which forms the walls of plant cells. Others are synthetic polymers, such as polyvinyl chloride (PVC) and nylon. A single polythene molecule consists of just two elements, carbon and hydrogen, but may contain up to 200,000 carbon atoms.

❹ SOLID SOLUTIONS

A solid solution is formed when atoms of one substance are distributed throughout those of another. Metal alloys can be solid solutions with the various metals melted and then allowed to solidify. Duralumin is a solid solution formed of 90 percent aluminum with copper, manganese, and magnesium. It is used in the aerospace industry because it is lightweight and very strong.

❺ SEPARATING MIXTURES

Many techniques have been developed to separate mixtures. Iron filings can be separated from sand by running a magnet over the mixture. This attracts the iron away from nonmagnetic sand. A centrifuge spins test tubes of material at high speed. Centrifuging relies on substances in a mixture possessing different densities. This causes different densities of liquid to separate into layers.

Centrifuge rotor spins, throwing the most dense substances to the bottom of the tubes

❻ DISTILLATION AND CHROMATOGRAPHY

When a liquid mixture is heated, the liquid with a lower boiling point becomes a vapor and can be hived off, leaving the other liquid behind. This is called distillation and it is used, for instance, to separate alcohol from water. Paper chromatography is used to separate mixtures of colored compounds, such as dyes or inks. Molecules in these substances have different properties and, when a solvent is applied, they travel at different speeds along paper, separating out.

The different substances show up as bands of different colors

❼ EVAPORATION

Evaporation is the process through which a liquid changes its state to a gas or vapor. It can be used to remove liquid from a solution, usually leaving behind a solid. The water in copper sulfate solution can be evaporated away to leave behind copper sulfate crystals. Cooking salt is produced in many warm regions by trapping seawater in large shallow pools. The water evaporates, leaving behind the salt, which is raked together into large mounds.

Salt pile from evaporated seawater. A liter of seawater contains around 1 oz (30 g) of salt.

ACIDS, BASES, AND SALTS

Acids and bases are chemical opposites, but they are closely related. Acids are substances that produce positively charged particles of hydrogen, called hydrogen ions (H^+) when dissolved in water. Bases are substances that can accept these hydrogen ions since they produce an excess of negatively charged particles called hydroxide ions (OH^-) in water. A base that is soluble in water is known as an alkali. Acids and bases are highly reactive with one another. They can be combined to produce many useful substances in the food, chemical, and metal industries.

❶ Indicators Different indicators can be used to measure how acidic or basic a substance is. Litmus paper turns red if it comes in contact with an acid and blue if it encounters an alkaline substance. A popular homemade indicator is red cabbage juice, which contains a substance called flavin. A strong base will turn the liquid greenish-yellow, while a strong acid will turn it red.

❷ Acids—sulfuric acid Sulfuric acid (H_2SO_4) is highly corrosive—capable of eating through metals. It is used as a drying agent to chemically remove water from many substances and is one of the most widely produced industrial chemicals in the world. This is because of its large number of uses, helping to produce fertilizers, dyes, drugs, paints, and dozens of other chemical products.

❸ Acids—vinegar The word acid comes from the Latin word *acidus*, meaning sour or sharp. Most acids, including vinegar (shown here), yogurt, and lemon juice, have a strong, sour taste. Table vinegar is mostly water, but gets its sour taste from acetic acid, which makes up around four to eight percent of its volume.

❹ pH scale pH stands for "power of hydrogen" and is a numbered scale running from close to zero (extremely acidic) to 14 (very heavily basic). It is a measure of the concentration of hydrogen ions in a substance. Pure water has a pH of seven, which is neutral—it is neither an acid nor a base. Each whole pH number on the scale is ten times more acidic or basic than the previous number.

❺ Bases and fats Bases tend to feel slippery and react with fats, such as butter, breaking them down so that they can be more easily washed away. As a result, bases are often used in strong household cleaners. For example, sodium hydroxide (NaOH), also known as caustic soda, is a powerful base used in the paper industry and is often the main active ingredient in drain unblockers and cleaners.

Butter can be broken down by bases

Acetic acid in vinegar is derived from ethanol

Lemon juice contains four to seven percent citric acid and has a pH between two and three

Hazard label for corrosive substances

Pure water has a pH of seven

❻ Acids—citric acid The sharp, tangy taste in some processed foods and soft drinks is due to the presence of a small amount of citric acid. Found naturally in citrus fruits, such as oranges, lemons, and limes, citric acid is used in the food industry and in many bathroom and kitchen cleaners. It is also found in water softeners that help soaps lather better.

❼ Saponification Reactions between certain acids and bases can result in the formation of soaps—a salt that comes from a fatty acid. This process is called saponification. Certain acidic substances, such as animal fats or olive oil (shown here), come from fatty acids. These can be hydrolyzed (broken down) by a strong base, such as sodium hydroxide, to form hard soaps or potassium hydroxide to form soft soaps.

❽ Batteries Both acids and bases can conduct electricity. The stronger the acid or base, the better it conducts. Both acids and bases are used widely in making batteries. One of the key substances inside an alkaline battery is the base, potassium hydroxide (KOH). Alkaline batteries tend to offer longer life than zinc chloride batteries of the same size.

❾ Salts—mercury sulfide Mercury sulfide (HgS) is a salt composed of mercury and sulfur. It is found in nature in two forms, a coarse, black powder called black mercuric sulfide, and a fine, bright-scarlet powder called red mercuric sulfide. The latter is used mainly as a coloring in art, where it is known as vermillion.

❿ Salts—potassium permanganate Potassium permanganate ($KMnO_4$) is a salt that dissolves in water to create intense purple-colored solutions. It is also soluble in sulfuric acid. It has a wide range of applications, including use in water treatment, as a disinfectant, as a fungicide, and as an industrial cleaner and bleacher.

⓫ Salts—copper sulfate Some acids and bases can react with each other to cancel out their acidic and basic properties—a reaction called neutralization. A neutralization reaction tends to produce a salt and water. An insoluble metal oxide can react with an acid to form a soluble salt. Sulfuric acid, for example, can react with copper(II) oxide to produce copper(II) sulfate with its distinctive blue color.

⓬ Bases—sodium bicarbonate A mild base with a pH of around eight, sodium bicarbonate ($NaHCO_3$) is used in cooking, where it reacts with acidic substances such as cocoa, yogurt, lemon juice, and buttermilk to generate carbon dioxide, which helps make dough rise. It is also found in many indigestion tablets to neutralize excess acid in the stomach.

Sodium bicarbonate can neutralize acidity of a bee sting

Blue copper(II) sulfate crystals created from copper(II) sulfate solution

Both types of mercury sulfide are insoluble in water

Potassium permanganate reacts with hydrochloric acid to create chlorine

Alkaline batteries

Lead-acid car battery contains sulfuric acid

79

MATERIALS SCIENCE

Humans have been working with materials for thousands of years, learning how to push them to their limits. Early civilizations discovered how to work clays into ceramics, make glass, and melt and work certain metals, such as iron, silver, tin, and copper. Modern scientists continue to develop more efficient methods of production or new uses for old materials, in addition to producing new materials with useful properties and applications.

▶ PROCESSING NATURAL MATERIALS

Many materials extracted from nature are in forms that require processing before use. For example, crude oil is heated in giant fractional distillation columns. Inside the columns, the crude oil separates into substances with different boiling points. These substances are called fractions. The fractions with the lowest boiling points, such as petroleum, rise to the top of the column, while those with higher boiling points, such as lubricating oil and bitumen, remain near the bottom.

More than 80 percent of all petroleum produced is used as fuel

▼ PLASTICS

Plastics produced from fractions of oil are one of the most common and versatile groups of materials. Most plastics will not react with other substances, making them useful as containers for potentially reactive liquids. Plastics can be produced that are light, waterproof, and good electrical and heat insulators. They can be formed into almost any shape, from thin sheet layers to complicated parts.

◀ PETROLEUM

When crude oil is processed using fractional distillation, one of the lightest fractions produced—petroleum—is also the most highly sought after. This liquid is consumed as a fuel for motor vehicles, but it has many other uses. It is also used to make detergents and many plastics. In the United States, 18.7 million barrels—each barrel containing 35 gallons (159 liters)—of petroleum was consumed in 2009 every day.

▶ BITUMEN

Bitumen is the heaviest fraction of crude oil produced by fractional distillation. It is a thick, oily substance with a boiling point of more than 977°F (525°C), and is used in many different waterproofing materials, including roofing felt. Bitumen asphalt is used in road surfacing, where it is rolled to form a smooth, hard-wearing surface.

▲ METAL ALLOYS

A metal alloy is a mixture of two or more metals, or a metal and other substances. Carbon is mixed with iron to form the world's most commonly used metal alloy, steel. Alloys have different properties from the original materials. Aluminum, for instance, is light in weight but relatively soft. It can be made harder by alloying it with other metals, such as copper.

▼ GLASSMAKING

Glass consists of silica from sand along with soda ash, limestone, and other substances. These are heated in a furnace during the manufacturing process. Glass can be shaped in many ways. It can be poured into molds, rolled into large, flat sheets, or blown into shape. Small amounts of other materials can be added to give glass different properties. When boron is added, it makes glass ovenproof, while the addition of lead can make glass more transparent.

Glassblowers shape the red-hot glass by blowing through a long tube

▼ MIXING IT UP

Composites combine the useful properties of two or more materials into one. Tiny carbon fibers are set into polymers, such as epoxy, polyester, and nylon. This creates materials that are extremely strong, but also lightweight. They are used extensively in the aerospace industry. The Model 281 Proteus is a high-altitude research aircraft built almost entirely of strong but light composite materials.

Carbon nanotubes can measure less than 1/50,000th the width of a human hair

The Proteus has a wingspan of 73 ft (22 m) but weighs just 5,887 lb (2,676 kg)

NANOTECHNOLOGY ▲

This involves producing and working with materials measured in nanometers, where a nanometer equals one-billionth of a meter. Scientists have managed to produce graphene—a layer of densely packed carbon atoms bonded together to form a sheet just one atom thick. Graphene can be rolled to form nanotubes. These are very strong materials that may have wide future applications in electronics and microscopic nanomachines.

Cutlery made from stainless steel, a steel alloy with chromium and nickel added

► SHAPE MEMORY ALLOYS

Advanced materials engineering has created metal alloys that remember their original shape after they have been bent, deformed, or stretched by heat. Shape Memory Alloys (SMAs) have many applications. For instance, more than half of all vascular stents (artificial tubes used in medicine to keep blood flowing through a blood vessel) are made from the SMA nitinol.

◄ RECYCLING

Collecting and reprocessing discarded materials to make new products and materials is called recycling. Aluminum drink cans, old glass bottles, and paper are commonly recycled. Every year, millions of worn-out car tires are discarded. Many are recycled by being shredded to produce a rubber crumb material. This can be used to produce shoe soles or playground surfaces.

IN A SPIN
A roller coaster transports thrill-seekers on a stomach-churning ride through multiple loops and spins. Different forces act on the cars and riders as they race along the twisting and turning track.

82

Energy and forces

Electric stove converts electrical energy into heat and light energy

❶ CHANGING FORMS

These runners are converting the chemical potential energy from food into kinetic energy (see below) as they run. Their movement also generates heat and sound energy. Many devices utilize electrical energy. This can be converted into kinetic energy in a fan, light in a lamp, or sound in a doorbell.

A tennis racket's strings, stretched by the ball, have potential energy

ENERGY

Energy is the ability to perform work. All living things need energy to survive and prosper. They obtain energy from food, which they digest and convert into substances that power their activity. Energy cannot be destroyed. It can, however, be transferred from one object to another, such as when a kicking foot transfers energy to a ball and moves it, or changed from one form of energy to another, such as when the physical movement of a strummed guitar string generates sound energy.

❷ KINETIC ENERGY

The energy something has because it is moving is known as kinetic energy. A stunt motorcyclist flying through the air has kinetic energy. The kinetic energy of an object depends on its speed and its mass. The greater an object's mass, and the faster it moves, the more kinetic energy it has.

❸ POTENTIAL ENERGY

Energy stored as a result of an object's chemistry, position, or state is potential energy. An object that is squashed, such as a spring, has potential energy. So does a tennis ball hit into the air. Its position above the ground, which required energy to achieve, gives it gravitational potential energy. As the ball falls, its potential energy changes back into kinetic energy.

Burning coal releases chemical energy originally created by prehistoric plants

An atomic bomb releases the same amount of energy as millions of tons of high explosives

Powerful fusion reactions occur in the Sun's core

❹ ELASTIC ENERGY

Elastic energy is potential energy stored in a compressed, stretched, or bent object. A pole vaulter in the middle of a vault grips a long flexible pole. It is almost bent in half due to its absorption of some of the athlete's kinetic energy from the run down the runway. As the pole straightens, its stored energy is released as kinetic energy, propelling the athlete upward and over the bar.

❺ CHEMICAL ENERGY

Much energy is stored in substances that can only release their energy as a result of a chemical reaction. Examples include the metabolism of food eaten by living things, the combustion of wood to generate heat and light, and the reaction of the chemicals in a battery to produce electrical energy.

❻ FUSION

Nuclear fusion is the joining together of the nuclei of atoms, which releases vast amounts of energy. It is how the Sun generates its energy. Research into nuclear fusion reactors promises a renewable form of energy in which 2.2 lb (1 kg) of hydrogen isotope fuel would generate the same amount of energy as 22 million lb (10 million kg) of fossil fuels.

❼ FISSION

Splitting the nuclei of atoms apart, in a process called nuclear fission, can release enormous amounts of energy. This has been used both as a devastating weapon and as a method of electricity generation. In a nuclear power plant, the nuclei of uranium-235 atoms are split to produce energy that drives electricity generators.

FORCES

From an apple falling to the ground to a car rolling to a halt, forces are constantly at work around us. Forces are pushes and pulls that act on an object. They can cause it to move or stop, speed up or slow down, or to change shape. Forces can be small and act locally or cause effects over vast distances, such as Earth's gravitational pull, which holds the Moon in its orbit at a distance of 238,900 miles (384,400 km).

The Moon is 2,173 miles (3,476 km) in diameter and has much less mass than the Earth

▼ FRICTION

When two things rub together, they create a force that opposes their movement. This is called friction. It occurs because no surfaces are perfectly uniform and smooth. This means that surfaces catch on each other. Friction allows shoes and bicycle tires to grip and push off the ground when moving. It also slows moving things down, can cause objects in contact to wear, and generates heat.

▲ GRAVITATIONAL PULL

The force of attraction between two objects is called gravity. When the objects have little mass, there is no noticeable effect, but when one object has great mass, such as the Earth, its gravity pulls objects to its surface. Objects dropped from a height accelerate at the same speed toward Earth—32.7 ft (9.8 m) per second per second—regardless of their mass. To lift an object, you must apply more force than the gravitational pull.

OVERCOMING FRICTION ▼

Friction can be reduced in several ways, such as by covering two moving surfaces with a thin layer of oil or powder—a process called lubrication. Rolling movement also reduces friction. A marble moves easily because a round surface constantly lifts off a flat surface so that less of their surface areas rub against each other.

Friction of brake blocks pressed onto wheel rim slows bike wheel down

◀ COMBINED FORCES

More than one force is often at work on a moving object at any one time. When two forces pull an object in opposite directions, the resultant force is found by subtracting the smaller force from the larger. A parachutist is pulled toward the ground by the force of gravity. As he travels through the air, his parachute creates a large amount of air resistance that slows his descent to the ground.

Helicopter rotor blades generate lift as they sweep through the air

▲ BALANCED FORCES

When you sit down on a chair, the force of your body weight is counteracted by the force of the chair pushing upward. The forces are balanced and you are said to be in equilibrium. Forces that are balanced cause no change in an object's speed or direction. A helicopter can hover in midair by balancing the forces of lift generated by its rotor blades with the force of gravity pulling it downward.

Pressure of the skate melts the ice, creating a thin layer of water for the skater to slide on

▲ FEEL THE SQUEEZE

Pressure describes force applied over a particular area. The amount of pressure generated depends on both the size of the force and the size of the area. A force acting over a small area will have a higher pressure than the same force acting over a larger area. The force of an ice skater's body weight is applied over the small area of the skate blade, which cuts into the ice.

▼ AIR RESISTANCE

Also known as drag, air resistance is the pushing of air against a moving object. Air and the object rub together, slowing the object down or making it use more energy to reach a certain speed. The faster an object moves, the greater the air resistance it encounters. Fast vehicles such as sports cars and jet aircraft are designed to be streamlined, which reduces drag.

Pointed nose helps channel air around vehicle

MOTION

Motion or movement is the change in location or position of an object over time. When an object moves, one or more forces are at work. Forces are measured in newtons (N), named after the British physicist Sir Isaac Newton (1642–1727). He formulated three laws of motion, which helped explain the principles of momentum and inertia, and the principle that for every action there is an equal and opposite reaction.

SPEED AND VELOCITY

The average speed of a sports car is determined by the distance it travels divided by the time taken. So, if the car completed a lap of 1.5 miles (2.4 km) in one minute, its average speed would be 90 mph (144 km/h). Velocity is a measure of speed in a particular direction. It changes if either the speed or direction of movement alters.

❷ ACCELERATION

As a car increases its straight-line speed and pulls away from vehicles behind it, it is said to accelerate. Acceleration is a change in velocity over time. Acceleration can be either an increase or decrease. Negative acceleration is sometimes called deceleration.

❸ INERTIA

Objects tend to move at the same speed and direction or, if at rest, stay at rest. A force has to be applied to overcome this inertia. A cyclist at a standstill must pedal hard to overcome the inertia that he and his bicycle possess. An object's inertia is determined by its mass. A supertanker has more inertia than a single-seat dinghy because it has greater mass and thus will require greater force to get it moving.

❹ MOMENTUM

When forces are balanced, a moving object keeps moving until another force stops it. The object is said to have momentum, which is measured as the velocity of an object multiplied by its mass. A soccer ball's momentum can be halted abruptly by a goalkeeper's hands exerting force to stop the ball.

❺ EQUAL AND OPPOSITE REACTION

Newton's third law of motion states that when one force acts on a body, an opposite action of equal force must occur. This is known as the reaction force. The jet engines on an airliner produce a powerful stream of hot gases flowing backward. These produce a reaction force of thrust that propels the airliner forward.

❻ TURNING FORCES

A pivot is a point, such as the hinges of a door, around which turning motion occurs. A turning force (also called a moment) is measured as the amount of force multiplied by the force's distance from the pivot point. The farther from the pivot the force is applied, the greater the turning force at the pivot. This is why a wrench is able to undo a tight nut and bolt with ease.

SIMPLE MACHINES

Simple machines are devices with a single part or a handful of parts that make it easier to perform work. Some simple machines, such as a pair of tweezers, allow people to be more precise when applying a force. Many others enable people to apply a force greater than their muscles can generate on their own. For example, a pole or tree branch can be used as a simple machine called a lever to move a heavy rock.

❶ INCLINED PLANES

An inclined plane, or ramp, is a simple machine consisting of a sloping surface. Like this builder's ramp up into a Dumpster, inclined planes are often used to help carry heavy loads. They can reduce the force required to raise an object by increasing the distance it travels. Some inclined planes, such as waterslides, work by allowing people and other objects to descend safely with less force than a vertical drop.

❷ WHEELS

One of humankind's greatest inventions, the wheel has enabled many forms of land transportation and machinery to flourish. A wheel turns around a shaft called an axle. When an axle is turned, the wheel turns with it. Since the wheel is much larger, it covers a greater distance than the axle. When the reverse is true, such as with a screwdriver, where the handle is the axle, the blade moves less distance than the axle but with greater force.

Load carried in wheelbarrow

❸ GEARS

Gears are toothed or grooved wheels that transmit a force from one place to another, or change the size or direction of a turning force. A bicycle chain allows the force of the turning chainwheel gear to be transmitted to a rear-wheel gear. A smaller rear-wheel gear in relation to the chainwheel turns more times than the chainwheel, but requires more force to turn it, and so is used for high speeds.

Axle of the chainwheel is turned by pedals

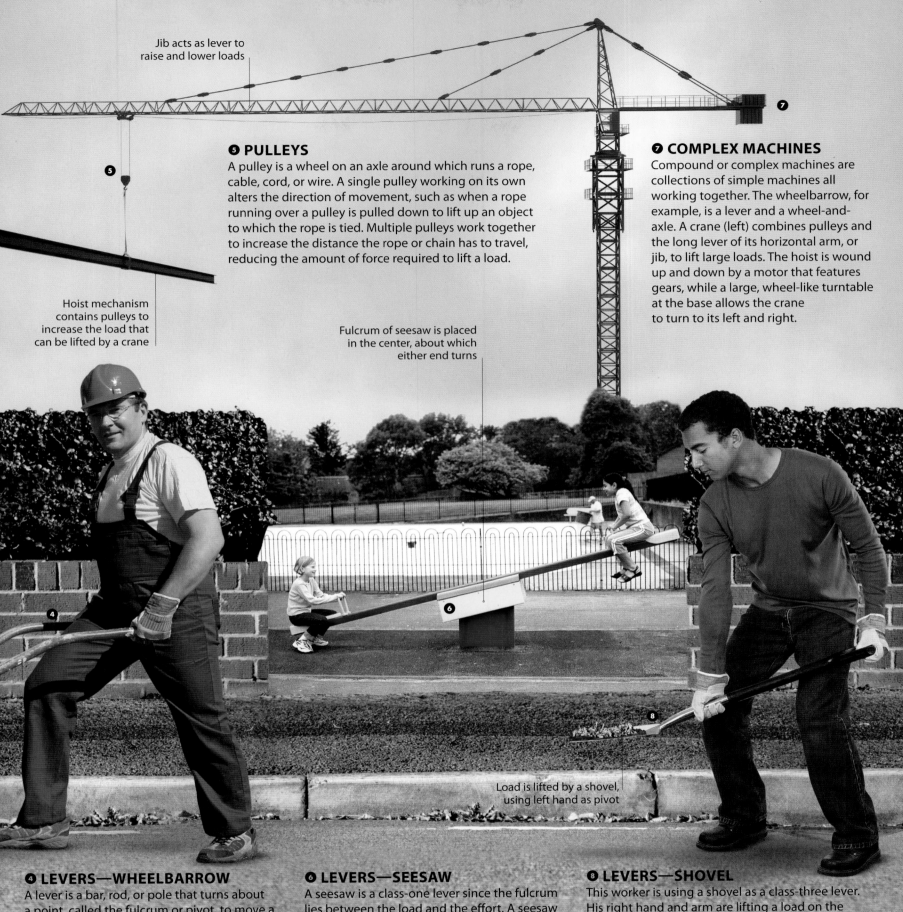

Jib acts as lever to
raise and lower loads

❺ PULLEYS

A pulley is a wheel on an axle around which runs a rope, cable, cord, or wire. A single pulley working on its own alters the direction of movement, such as when a rope running over a pulley is pulled down to lift up an object to which the rope is tied. Multiple pulleys work together to increase the distance the rope or chain has to travel, reducing the amount of force required to lift a load.

❼ COMPLEX MACHINES

Compound or complex machines are collections of simple machines all working together. The wheelbarrow, for example, is a lever and a wheel-and-axle. A crane (left) combines pulleys and the long lever of its horizontal arm, or jib, to lift large loads. The hoist is wound up and down by a motor that features gears, while a large, wheel-like turntable at the base allows the crane to turn to its left and right.

Hoist mechanism
contains pulleys to
increase the load that
can be lifted by a crane

Fulcrum of seesaw is placed
in the center, about which
either end turns

Load is lifted by a shovel,
using left hand as pivot

❹ LEVERS—WHEELBARROW

A lever is a bar, rod, or pole that turns about a point, called the fulcrum or pivot, to move a load. The positions of the effort, load, and fulcrum of the lever vary and give rise to three groups of levers, called classes. A wheelbarrow is an example of a class-two lever because the load (of bricks) sits between the effort (lifting the handles of the wheelbarrow) and the fulcrum (the wheel).

❻ LEVERS—SEESAW

A seesaw is a class-one lever since the fulcrum lies between the load and the effort. A seesaw is unusual in that the load and effort are approximately the same distance away from the fulcrum, allowing the children to move up and down using their weight as effort. Most class-one levers, such as scissors, magnify force by moving the point of effort a greater distance away from the fulcrum than the load.

❽ LEVERS—SHOVEL

This worker is using a shovel as a class-three lever. His right hand and arm are lifting a load on the shovel's blade. The shovel pivots around the handle held with his left hand. A class-three lever has the effort close to the load and on the same side of the fulcrum as the load. Your forearms are class-three levers since the effort is provided by your biceps, the load is your hand, and the fulcrum is your elbow joint.

ELECTROMAGNETIC SPECTRUM

The colors you can see make up the visible light spectrum. Visible light, however, is just one of a number of forms of energy that travel in waves at a speed of 186,000 miles (300,000 km) per second. This is the speed of light. These differing forms of energy, from radio waves to gamma rays, are together called the electromagnetic spectrum. All, except visible light, are invisible to the naked eye, but their effects can be observed and studied. Some carry more energy than others, and the different wavelengths of energy exhibit different properties. They all have been harnessed and put to work in a variety of applications.

❶ WAVELENGTH

Each type of wave in the electromagnetic spectrum has its own wavelength. This is the distance between two identical parts of a wave, such as two peaks or two troughs. Wavelengths range from many meters for long radio waves down to one-billionth of a meter for gamma rays. Frequency is the rate at which waves pass a given point. Visible light frequencies range from 430 trillion waves per second for the color red up to 750 trillion waves per second for violet.

❷ GAMMA RAYS

Created through the radioactive decay of atoms, gamma waves have the shortest wavelength of all electromagnetic waves, often smaller than single atoms, and possess extremely high energy. Harmful to humans in large quantities, their controlled use is deployed to sterilize medical instruments and to attack cancers. Scanners using gamma rays can see through metals to check for cracks and faults in aircraft bodies or to search metal cargo containers for stowaways and security risks.

Gamma rays are used in this security scan of a truck at a border crossing

❸ X-RAYS

Since they were first discovered by accident in a laboratory experiment by German scientist Wilhelm Conrad Röntgen (1845–1923), X-rays have been investigated and used heavily in medicine. X-rays can penetrate flesh but are absorbed by more dense substances such as bone, teeth, and metals. They allow images of the inside the body to be taken for diagnosis. X-rays are used to examine pipelines for defective joints and to discover paintings hidden under other artworks.

A 16th-century painting x-rayed by art restorers yields clues to how it was produced

Gamma ray

X-ray

Ultraviolet

Visible

Wavelength

Infrared

Microwave

Radio

4 ULTRAVIOLET

With a wavelength just shorter than the visible light spectrum, ultraviolet (UV) rays have various uses. When UV rays fall on certain substances, the substances fluoresce, or emit visible light. UV watermarks on these bank notes (right) help prevent forgery, while police and forensics teams use ultraviolet lighting to detect small amounts of blood.

5 INFRARED RAYS

Between visible light and microwaves exists infrared radiation. It is given off by all warm things, from stars to the heat lamps used to treat sports injuries. Infrared photography builds up a heat picture and is used to detect defects in electronics. Infrared with wavelengths close to red in the spectrum give off little heat and are used in many short-range remote controls.

TV remote works using infrared rays

6 RADIO WAVES

This model buggy is remote-controlled, using radio waves to send and receive signals. Radio waves have the longest wavelength in the spectrum, from about 4 in (10 cm) up to hundreds of meters or longer. They are used for a wide range of wireless communication, including TV, radio, and Wi-Fi wireless computer networking.

Radio antenna picks up radio waves from controller

7 VISIBLE LIGHT

The visible light spectrum consists of electromagnetic waves that human beings can see. A rainbow, caused by sunlight striking moisture in the air at certain angles, depicts all the colors of visible light. Each color has a different wavelength, with red possessing the longest and violet the shortest. When all the waves are seen together, they make white light.

8 MICROWAVES

Very short radio waves called microwaves have a wide range of communication uses, from sending and receiving global positioning system (GPS) signals to transmitting radar. Hands-free receivers (left) use microwaves to enable wireless mobile phone communication. A microwave oven bombards food with rays. This makes the water molecules in the food vibrate, generating heat that cooks the food from the inside out.

Hands-free earpiece receives microwaves from a mobile phone

A humpback whale's song can travel more than 60 miles (100 km) through water.

A space shuttle liftoff generates a sound level of 180 decibels.

SOUND

When you hit a drum, you generate energy waves that vibrate and travel away from the source of the sound, gradually losing their force as they ripple outward. A sound needs a source to generate it, as well as a medium—a substance that carries sound. It also needs a receiver, such as the human ear, to detect the sound. Sounds above the level of human hearing are called ultrasound. This is used in medicine, for example, where ultrasound scanners provide diagnostic images of the body's internal organs.

▲ SPEED OF SOUND

The speed at which sound travels varies and depends on the density of the medium. At sea level, sound travels through air at a speed of 1,115 ft/s (340 m/s). This speed drops to 980 ft/s (300 m/s) at an altitude of 33,000 ft (10,000 m), where air is less dense. In a dense medium, such as the closely packed molecules of water, sound travels faster—at about 3,800 ft/s (1,500 m/s).

▲ AMPLITUDE

The measure of a sound's intensity—how much energy it has—is called amplitude. The more energy a sound wave has, the greater the peaks in its wave, and the louder the sound will seem. The decibel scale is used to describe the loudness of sounds, from a quiet whisper of about 30 decibels to a jackhammer digging up roads at about 115 decibels. Each rise of 10 decibels on the scale means the sound is ten times louder.

▼ FREQUENCY AND PITCH

A sound's frequency is measured in hertz (Hz)—the number of vibrations the sound makes in one second. The greater the frequency of a sound, the more vibrations it makes per second and the higher the pitch of the sound. Human hearing has a broad range, from low sounds of 20 Hz up to high-pitched sounds of 20,000 Hz (20 kHz). As we get older, our range of hearing decreases. Some animals, such as dogs, can detect sounds higher than 45 kHz, while bats can detect sounds up to 120 kHz.

The hole behind the strings provides an opening to the guitar's sound box.

▲ GOOD VIBRATIONS

The sound waves from many musical instruments vibrate through a solid material, such as wood, and the air. The strings of an acoustic guitar, for example, create sound waves in the air. The strings do not disturb a great deal of air and so, by themselves, do not create a loud sound. But the vibrations also travel through the guitar's body—the sound box. This amplifies the sound before it leaves via the sound hole.

◀ REFLECTING AND ABSORBING

Smooth, hard surfaces tend to reflect sound, making the waves change direction. An echo—when a sound is made, then reflected back—has a delay because the sound waves have to travel outward and back. Echoes are often fainter because only some of the sound waves are reflected—the remainder are absorbed by the material. Certain soft materials, such as foam, are good at absorbing sound waves.

Acoustic foam helps absorb sound waves and is used in recording studios.

▶ MICROPHONE

A microphone converts sounds into electrical signals. These can then be recorded, processed, or sent to an amplifier to have the sound's amplitude increased before being broadcast. There are various types of microphones. Inside this condenser model, sound waves vibrate a flexible diaphragm. The diaphragm is part of an electrical component called a capacitor. This generates a variable electrical signal depending on the position of the diaphragm.

▼ LOUDSPEAKER

Electrical signals from an instrument or a stereo reach a loudspeaker's metal coil, turning it into an electromagnet that produces a fluctuating magnetic field. This field causes a diaphragm joined to a paper or plastic cone to move back and forth. The vibrating movement creates sound waves that reproduce and amplify the original sounds. A loudspeaker cabinet often contains more than one speaker, with a tweeter to reproduce high sounds and a woofer for low-pitched sounds.

▼ RESONANCE

Most solid objects have a natural frequency or group of frequencies at which they vibrate. This is their resonant frequency. If a sound of the same frequency is made near an object, it can pick up energy from the sound wave and vibrate itself. A crystal wine glass can vibrate at its resonant frequency to the point that the glass bends too far, then cracks and shatters.

Wine glass shatters when a loud sound is equal to its resonant frequency

HEAT

Heat is a form of energy. It is often measured in calories or joules. A calorie is the amount of heat required to raise the temperature of 1 gram of water by 1°C. One calorie is equal to 4.1855 joules. Heat is transferred from one body to another because of a difference in temperature. Heat tends to move from a warmer area to a colder one. Heat can also alter the state a substance is in. If enough heat is applied to a solid, for example, it begins to melt and change state into a liquid.

▲ RADIATION

Energetic particles traveling in waves transmit energy by radiation (see pages 92–93). Infrared radiation is thermal (heat) radiation transmitted by warm and hot objects. The hotter the object, the more energy it gives out. The hottest object of all in our Solar System, the Sun, warms Earth through vast amounts of infrared radiation.

Balloon envelope is filled with hot air so balloon rises

▲ EXPANDING AND CONTRACTING

Increasing heat can cause substances to expand in volume. Air heated by a hot-air balloon burner expands to fill the balloon's envelope. The hot air is less dense than the surrounding cold air. As a result, the hot air rises, carrying the balloon with it. A decrease in heat causes substances to contract. Large structures, such as bridges, contain expansion joints to buffer the expansion and contraction of the structure's materials that occur as the temperature changes.

▼ MEASURING HEAT

Temperature is a measurement of how fast the molecules in an object are moving. Thermometers measure temperature. Some rely on liquid mercury in a small reservoir, which expands and rises up a graduated scale when warmer and contracts and drops down the scale when cooler. Others are electronic, using thermistors to measure electrical resistance, which increases with a rise in temperature. Temperature can be described using one of several different temperature scales.

The Celsius scale measures temperature in 100 units between the freezing point (0°C) and boiling point (100°C) of water

120°F on the Fahrenheit scale is equal to 48.89°C

Hang gliders soar on circulating convection currents of warm air

◀ CONVECTION

Heat can be transferred through the process of convection, in which it is carried through a liquid, air, or another gas. If air is heated, its molecules spread out, it lowers in density, and as a result, it rises. Cooler air flows in to take its place and will become warmed itself, while the warmer air will lose its heat and begin to sink. This pattern of warming and cooling creates circulating convection currents in the air.

Warm clothes, like this down jacket, trap layers of warm air close to the body, slowing heat loss

◀ INSULATORS

A substance that does not let heat travel through it easily is known as an insulator. In many situations, we want to trap heat and stop or slow its flow. Plastic, rubber, and wood are good insulators and are often used for saucepan handles to keep heat from the pan from flowing up to burn the cook's hand. Air is also a good insulator. Animal fur traps warm air close to the creature's skin to keep it warm.

Heat conducts easily and evenly through a metal saucepan to boil water quickly

◀ CONDUCTION

This is the transfer of heat through matter from particle to particle, molecule to molecule. Solids tend to be better conductors than gases since their molecules are more closely packed together. As the molecules nearest the heat source gain energy and increase their vibration, they pass on some of their energy to neighboring molecules. Metals are very good heat conductors and are used in saucepans, soldering irons, and heating elements in stoves.

LIGHT

Lying between infrared and ultraviolet waves on the electromagnetic spectrum, visible light consists of electromagnetic waves mostly emitted by warm objects such as the Sun or a light bulb. Some chemical reactions, such as combustion, can also generate light. Nothing travels faster than light, which moves in straight lines, spreading out over an increasingly large area, and diminishing in power over distance. Unlike sound waves, light can travel through a vacuum.

▲ LETTING LIGHT THROUGH

Some materials, such as the glass of this window, are transparent. They let almost all light through. Opaque materials, such as wood and metals, are those that do not let light through. Translucent materials, such as some camera lens filters and tissue paper, let some light through, but scatter the waves in all directions.

▼ REFRACTION

Light travels through different materials, or media, at different speeds. For example, it travels a little more slowly through water and glass than through air. Refraction occurs when light bends as a result of changing speed as it passes from one medium to another. Swimming pools, for example, tend to look more shallow from the side than they really are. The light from the bottom of the pool bends as it leaves the water.

▲ LASERS

When the atoms inside a laser are excited by an energy source, they give off photons (particles of light). All the photons have the same amount of energy, which means that lasers produce a highly concentrated beam of light of just one wavelength. Laser light can travel great distances with little weakening or spreading. Lasers are used in a huge range of applications, from concert lighting to satellite communications.

Refraction of the light means that the straw looks bent where it enters the water

Concave lenses help correct myopia (nearsightedness)

A disco ball's flat shiny mirrors reflect light

White light passing through a transparent prism separates out into differing color wavelengths

COLOR ▶

Within the spectrum of visible light lie different wavelengths that exhibit different colors. Red has the longest wavelength and violet the shortest. When light strikes a colored object, the object absorbs the other colors, but reflects its color back. The red light on a traffic light glows red because the red filter absorbs all the other colors from its white lamp, but lets red through.

▲ REFLECTION

When light strikes an object, its rays can be either absorbed or reflected. A solid black object absorbs almost all light, while a shiny, smooth surface, such as a mirror, reflects almost all light back. When reflected off a flat mirror, light bounces off at an angle equal to the angle at which it struck the mirror. A rough surface tends to bounce rays off at different angles, scattering the light.

▼ ELECTRIC LIGHT

Electrical energy can be converted into light energy in a number of different ways. In an incandescent light bulb, an electric current passes through a thin filament, often made of tungsten, which is heated and glows, producing light. Incandescent bulbs are gradually being replaced by more reliable and efficient lights, including Compact Fluorescent Lamps (CFLs). When electricity passes through the gases in a CFL, they give off ultraviolet light, which causes the lamp's phosphor coating to glow.

◀ LENSES

Transparent, curved, polished surfaces called lenses alter the direction of light waves. A wide range of applications in optics and photography use lenses. Convex lenses have thicker centers than edges. Waves passing through a convex lens converge (come together). Convex lenses are used to magnify images. A concave lens has a thinner center than edges, and spreads out, or diverges, light passing through it.

ELECTRICITY

Few forms of energy have a greater impact on our lives than electricity. All materials consist of positive and negative charges. These are normally balanced out in most atoms, leaving the atom electrically neutral. Electricity is made when electrons are free to jump from one atom to another, while the nucleus of the atom remains still. This can occur in lightning, electrical gadgets, and through nerves racing between your eye and brain as you read this.

▶ CURRENT ELECTRICITY

An electric current is a flow of electric charge. Unless there is a continuous, unbroken loop for electrons to flow through, an electric current cannot be sustained. An electrical switch in a circuit can break or complete a loop, stopping a current or allowing it to travel through a circuit. The number of electrons that pass a given point in an electrical circuit at one time is measured in amperes, or amps.

▶ INSULATORS

Electrical insulators are the opposite of conductors. Their electrons are tightly bound in their atoms and are not free to roam and flow from one atom to another. Common electrical insulators are glass, rubber, plastic, wood, and ceramic. Plastic coatings cover most electrical wires in appliances, while ceramic and rubber insulation may be used in power lines to protect people from the danger of high-voltage electricity.

◀ STATIC

When substances have a surplus of positive or negative charges, they will attempt to stay balanced by attracting one another. If you rub your hands on a balloon, for example, a surplus of electrical charges builds up on the surface of the balloon and on your body. The charges remain static (still) until they find a way to escape. If static charge builds up on the surface of your hair, it will stand on end. The hairs all have the same charge, which makes them repel one another.

Static-electricity buildup causes hairs to stand on end

▼ RESISTANCE

A measure of how much something resists the free flow of electric current is called resistance. Good conductors have low resistance, while insulators have very high resistance. Resistors add a deliberate amount of resistance to an electrical circuit. They can be fixed—set at a particular resistance—or variable. A variable resistor changes the amount of resistance when, for example, a person adjusts a control.

Volume control attached to a variable resistor

▲ CONDUCTORS

Electric current can only pass through materials that allow the free flow of electrons. These materials are called conductors. Metals, especially silver, are good conductors of electricity. Copper, which is cheaper than silver, is made into millions of miles of electrical wire every year. Semiconductors, which can carry a current, but not as easily as a conductor, are used to make devices such as transistors. These are used to amplify or switch electrical signals.

▼ CIRCUIT DIAGRAMS

When an electrical power source, such as a battery, is attached to a complete circuit, electrons flow from its negative terminal around the circuit to its positive terminal. An electrical circuit channels or modifies the flow of electricity to perform a task, with some components converting electrical energy to heat, light, sound, or movement.

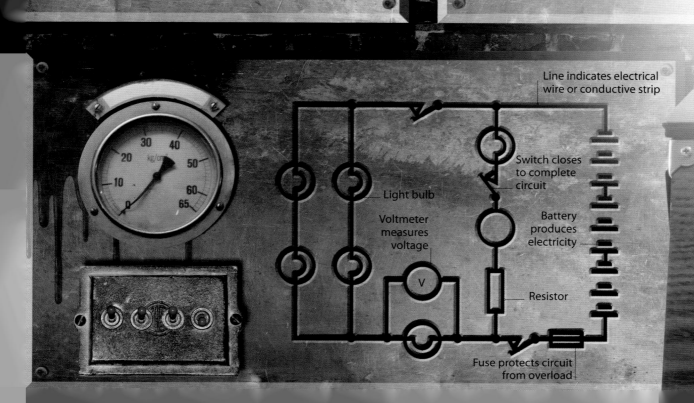

Line indicates electrical wire or conductive strip

Light bulb

Voltmeter measures voltage

Switch closes to complete circuit

Battery produces electricity

Resistor

Fuse protects circuit from overload

MAGNETISM

Magnetism is a force that can attract (pull toward) or repel (push away) some materials. Certain elements, such as cobalt, iron, and nickel, are strongly attracted by a magnetic force and are called ferromagnetic. These materials' atoms line up readily in the same direction. Elements that are attracted by magnets can also be turned into magnets. A steel rod stroked repeatedly with a magnet will generate its own magnetic force.

▶ ELECTROMAGNETS AT WORK

This giant electromagnet fitted to a crane can lift and drop waste metal around a scrap yard at the press of a button. Electromagnets are found in many devices, from magnetic door locks to loudspeakers. Magnetic levitation (maglev) trains use the repelling power of magnets to keep a train hovering about 0.4 in (10 mm) above its track. With no friction between moving parts, maglev trains can move at very high speeds.

Heavy steel girder
lifted high by
electromagnet

▼ ELECTRIC MOTORS

Electricity flows through the armature coil of a simple electric motor, turning the armature into an electromagnet with its own north and south poles. These interact with one or more fixed magnets around the inside of the motor's case, called the stator. As the armature repeatedly moves to align its magnetic poles with the other magnets, it rotates, turning the motor's axle.

Electric motor axle is connected to armature inside motor

Current flows through wire coil, generating a magnetic field

▶ REPEL AND ATTRACT

The two ends of a magnet are called its north and south poles. If a long bar magnet is cut in half, each half becomes a complete magnet, with a north and south pole. When a north and a south pole from two magnets face each other, they are attracted toward each other. When like poles of two magnets are placed close to one another, they repel or push away from each other.

The same poles of two bar magnets repel each other

▶ MAGNETIC FIELDS

The area of space around a magnet where magnetism is detected is called a magnetic field. The poles are where the magnetic field is at its strongest. The larger and more powerful the magnet, the greater its magnetic field. A wire carrying an electric current generates a magnetic field around the wire.

Iron filings show the pattern of a magnetic field around a bar magnet

▶ ELECTROMAGNETISM

An electromagnet is created by running an electric current through a coil of wire to generate a magnetic field. The coil is often wound around an iron core, but can be doughnut-shaped with a core of air, which is called a solenoid. The strength of an electromagnet can be altered by changing the amount of electric current that flows through it.

Compass needle points north, allowing navigation

▶ MAGNETIC EARTH

Electric currents in Earth's core generate a magnetic field. It is at its strongest at the magnetic North and South Poles (which are near to but not at the geographical North and South Poles). This magnetic field extends out into space, where it is known as the magnetosphere. A compass uses a magnet on a pivot whose north-seeking pole points to magnetic north.

CLOUDS OF CREATION
Gigantic clouds of gas and dust, the raw materials for building new stars and creating new solar systems, form the beautiful Orion Nebula, which lies about 1,500 light years from Earth.

Space

THE UNIVERSE

The Universe contains everything. It includes all known matter, from the smallest atomic particle to the largest galaxy. Scientists estimate that there are around 10^{21} (1,000,000,000,000,000,000,000) stars in the Universe. Yet most of it is made up of vast distances of space between celestial bodies. Cosmology is the study of the Universe, how it began, how it developed, and what might happen to it in the future.

▶ THE BIG BANG ▶

No one knows for certain how the Universe originated or what, if anything, came before. The current theory is that around 13.7 billion years ago, the Universe, space, and time expanded very rapidly out of a single point. In a tiny fraction of a second, cosmic inflation saw the Universe grow at an unbelievably fast rate. Within minutes, radiating energy turned into particles of matter.

▶ COOLING DOWN, HEATING UP

Over a period of about 300,000 years, the Universe continued to expand and cool. Near the end of this period, the first stable atoms formed from hydrogen and helium nuclei, joining with protons and electrons. Gravity pulled gases into clouds that heated up, binding particles together, and forming the earliest stars and galaxies.

◀ LIGHT-YEARS

Astronomers need larger measurements than miles and kilometers to convey the immense distances in space. Light travels at about 186,000 miles (300,000 km) per second. So the distance it travels in a year is 5.9 trillion miles (9.5 trillion km). This distance is called a light-year.

Proxima Centauri is the nearest star to our Solar System. It is about 4.22 light-years away

▶ SEEING THE PAST

When astronomers observe an object at huge distances, they are looking back deep into the past because of the millions of years it takes light to travel across the Universe. A galaxy viewed at a distance of 2 billion light-years is seen as it was 2 billion years ago. In 2010, galaxy UDFy-38135539 (right) was detected. It is more than 13 billion light-years away.

This galaxy is the most distant and earliest

In a few trillionths of a second, the Universe expanded from a single point to the size of a galaxy

▶ THE UNIVERSE TODAY

The Universe today is still expanding and is believed to be more than 90 billion light-years in diameter. What astronomers can detect using scientific instruments is only part of the story. Much of the Universe is hidden from us as dark energy and dark matter. These mysterious phenomena are invisible to telescopes but their effects, such as their gravitational pull on stars, galaxies, and light, can be observed.

▶ LIFE ELSEWHERE?

Humans are fascinated by the possibility of life elsewhere in the Universe. The vast distances of space prevent a physical search far beyond our Solar System—the *Pioneer 10* probe launched in 1972, for example, will take about two million years to reach the star Aldebaran. Instead, astronomers use telescopes to find exoplanets (planets outside the Solar System).

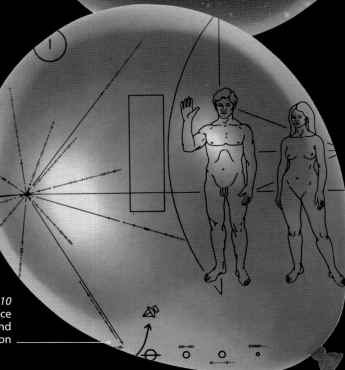

Plaque on *Pioneer 10* probe sent into deep space depicts adult humans and Earth's location

◀ FATE OF THE UNIVERSE

No-one is sure how the Universe will end. The open Universe theory is that it will continue to expand for ever, with the stars and galaxies dying out and space becoming a cold, dark waste. The flat Universe theory proposes that its expansion will slow to a point where the forces of expansion and gravity are balanced. The third theory, the closed Universe, is explained below.

Open Universe

Flat Universe

Closed Universe
(see below)

Separation between galaxies

Big Bang

Time

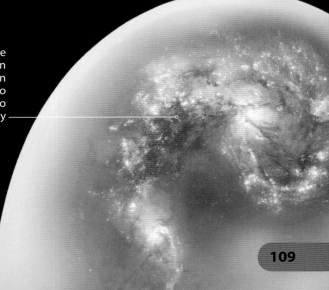

The Antennae Galaxies began colliding more than 700 million years ago and are merging into one large galaxy

▶ WHEN GALAXIES COLLIDE

The closed Universe theory suggests that the Universe will stop expanding and will start to pull back on itself. This would cause galaxies to collide and condense inward, until the entire Universe had shrunk into one unimaginably large black hole—the so-called Big Crunch. Whether the Universe is expanding or contracting, the forces of gravity will cause galaxies to collide.

GALAXIES AND STARS

Stars are fiercely burning balls of gas with powerful nuclear reactions at their cores. Around 5,000 stars are potentially viewable from Earth with the naked eye, but billions more exist, many of which have been cataloged and classified by astronomers. Despite the vast distances separating most stars from each other, they are bound by gravity into massive systems called galaxies. Galaxies also include star remains, gas, and dust. There are at least 125 billion galaxies in the Universe and potentially many more.

▶ STARS

Astronomers group stars into seven spectral types based on the temperature they burn at. Type O are the hottest, followed by B, A, F, G, K, and M, the coolest. The Sun is a type G star, while Rigel (right) is a type B star about 700–900 light-years away from Earth. Rigel shines many thousands of times more brightly than the Sun.

▶ SPIRAL GALAXIES

Shaped like a disk, spiral galaxies often have a bulge in the center and curved arms that spiral outward as the galaxy rotates. The Milky Way is a type of spiral galaxy, as is NGC 1309 (right), a galaxy three-quarters the size of the Milky Way and about 120 million light-years away. Even bigger is the Andromeda Galaxy. It is 220,000 light-years in diameter and may contain a trillion stars.

▶ THE MILKY WAY

The Solar System resides in the Orion arm of the Milky Way galaxy. The Milky Way is a spinning barred spiral galaxy about 100,000 light-years in diameter, but only between 1,000 and 4,000 light-years thick. Our Sun lies about 25,000 light-years from the center of the galaxy and is just one of 200–500 billion stars that are found in this galaxy.

◀ MAGNITUDE

Astronomers measure and classify stars in a number of ways. One of the most basic measures is apparent magnitude—the brightness of a star as viewed from Earth. The Sun, as the brightest object in the sky, has an apparent magnitude of -26.8, while the next three brightest stars are Sirius (-1.6), Canopus (-0.7), and Alpha Centauri (0.1). The least bright stars viewed with an optical telescope from Earth have a magnitude of around 30.

◀▶ GALAXY TYPES

Astronomers classify galaxies by their overall shape. Many galaxies are oval-shaped ellipticals, or spirals, like Andromeda (right). Lenticular galaxies are flat disks often with a central bulge. They are believed to contain few newborn stars and mainly older, mature stars. NGC 5886 (left) is a lenticular galaxy some 45 million light-years away and is viewed edge-on from Earth. Around one in four galaxies are classed as irregular since they appear to lack a particular shape or form. This may be due to gravity from neighboring galaxies pulling them out of shape. Most irregular galaxies contain a large amount of dust, gas, and infant stars. NGC 4449 (above) is an irregular galaxy 12 million light-years from Earth. Its reddish areas are star-forming regions.

▶ GALAXY CLUSTERS

Galaxies often exist as part of a collection known as a cluster. The Milky Way exists in a cluster called the Local Group along with Andromeda, Canis Major Dwarf, Triangulum, Pisces, and more than 40 other galaxies. A number of the members of the Local Group are dwarf galaxies that have only been discovered in recent years. The Local Group is estimated to have a diameter of around 10 million light-years.

◀ SUPERCLUSTERS

A supercluster is a number of galaxy clusters grouped together. Our local supercluster, the Virgo Supercluster, contains as many as 100 galaxy clusters, making it a staggering 100 million light-years in size. Other superclusters, such as Perseus-Pisces, more than 180 million light-years away, are thought to be three times larger.

THE SOLAR SYSTEM

Our Solar System is dominated by a fiery star at its center, the Sun. This contains 99.8 percent of the entire system's mass. Asteroids, planets, and other objects, drawn by the Sun's great gravitational pull, travel on elliptical paths around it, taking varying periods of time to complete an orbit. The dwarf planet Pluto takes 248 Earth years to complete a circuit of the Sun, while Mercury orbits the Sun in just 88 Earth days.

▼ THE PLANETS

Eight major planets orbit the Sun. Neptune is the farthest away, as far as 2.84 billion miles (4.54 billion km). Mercury, the smallest planet, is the closest at 29 million miles (46 million km). As a result, temperatures on its surface can soar above 800°F (430°C). Yet Venus, shrouded in its thick insulating atmosphere, is thought to be the hottest planet at around 870°F (465°C). The fastest winds in the Solar System are found in Neptune's atmosphere, where storms rage at speeds of more than 1,300 mph (2,100 km/h).

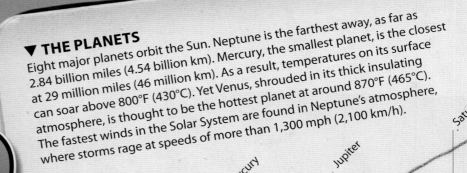

Sun · Mercury · Venus · Earth · Mars · Jupiter · Saturn

Gaspra measures just 11.5 miles (18.5 km) across

▲ ASTEROID BELT

Asteroids are chunks of rock and metal that orbit the Sun. More than 9 out of 10 asteroids are found in a belt lying between Mars and Jupiter. Many astronomers believe they are the remains of a planet that failed to form. The largest asteroid, Ceres, measures 609 miles (974 km) in diameter, but the vast majority are much smaller.

◄ ROCKY WORLDS

The four inner planets, Mercury, Venus, Earth, and Mars, have metal inner cores and rocky crusts. Mars's red color (left) comes from its soil, which is rich in iron oxide. The Venusian atmosphere consists mainly of carbon dioxide with some sulfur dust and sulfuric acid droplets. Like our Moon, the surface of Mercury is heavily cratered.

The dwarf planet Eris, with the Sun in the distance

Uranus

Neptune

▼ GAS GIANTS

All four of the outer planets are giant balls of gas. They lack a solid outer surface, but are believed to possess a solid core. These gas giants dwarf the four rocky planets. The largest, Jupiter, is 88,846 miles (142,984 km) across—more than 11 times the diameter of Earth. All four gas giants have rings of matter, although Saturn's (below) are the most pronounced.

◄ KUIPER BELT

The Kuiper belt stretches out like a giant disk past Neptune and deep into space. It contains thousands of rocky or icy objects, many of which are 30–60 miles (50–100 km) in diameter. It includes dwarf planets such as Pluto. A new dwarf planet, Eris, was discovered in the belt in 2005. Measuring approximately 1,550 miles (2,500 km) across, its current location places it on an orbital path roughly three times farther away from the Sun than Pluto.

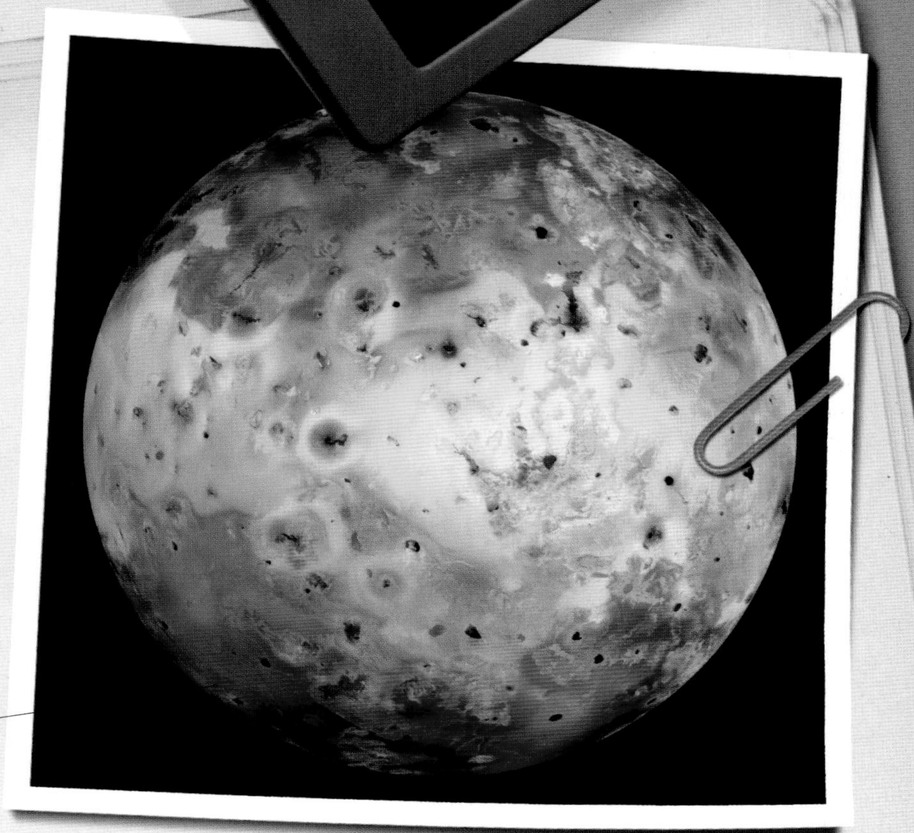

Io's surface is covered with the scars of volcanic eruptions

▲ NATURAL SATELLITES

More than 160 natural satellites or moons exist in the Solar System, each orbiting a planet. Mars has two, Phobos and Deimos, while Saturn and Jupiter both have more than 60 moons. Ganymede, which orbits Jupiter, is the largest at 3,293 miles (5,268 km) in diameter and is bigger than the planet Mercury. A number of moons interest astronomers greatly. These include Io (above), which is the most volcanically active body in the Solar System, and Triton, Neptune's largest moon, which has a crust of solid frozen nitrogen.

SUN AND MOON

The Sun is our closest star and the Moon is our nearest celestial neighbor. The Sun has a diameter of about 865,000 miles (1.392 million km), more than 109 times the diameter of Earth. This giant sphere of intensely hot gases generates phenomenal amounts of energy at its core. The energy travels through the Sun's layers and out into the Solar System, warming our planet and enabling life to flourish.

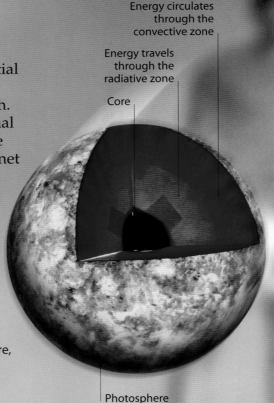

Energy circulates through the convective zone

Energy travels through the radiative zone

Core

Photosphere

▶ SUN STRUCTURE

The Sun consists of a number of layers, beginning with an extremely dense yet still gaseous core, which spans about a quarter of the Sun's diameter. Energy passes through and around the convective and radiative zones of the Sun before reaching the photosphere, which has a thickness of about 300 miles (500 km). This is the Sun's surface, where temperatures average 10,300°F (5,700°C). Beyond the photosphere lies the hotter inner atmosphere, or chromosphere, and finally the corona, the outer atmosphere.

◀ SOLAR FURNACE

Hydrogen makes up almost three-quarters of the mass of the Sun. The rest is mostly helium. Vast pressures and temperatures of millions of degrees in the core cause nuclear fusion reactions. These convert hydrogen atoms into helium—with incredible amounts of energy generated as a result.

Hydrogen

Hydrogen

Helium

▼ SPOTS AND FLARES

Sunspots are areas of the Sun's surface that are cooler than the surrounding regions and are caused by interference from the Sun's own magnetic field. A sunspot recorded in 2003 (below, bottom) was the diameter of 15 Earths. A solar flare is an enormous explosion of energy from the Sun's surface.

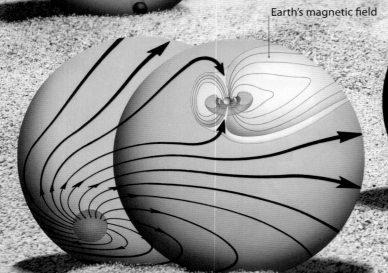

Earth's magnetic field

Largest sunspot seen by SOHO probe

▲ SOLAR WIND

A stream of particles is continually ejected from the Sun. These carry strong electrical and magnetic fields as they billow out across the Solar System. Earth's own magnetic field (above) is shaped by the solar wind, extending away from the Sun in a teardrop shape.

▲ STUDYING THE SUN

One of the most successful solar probes has been SOHO—the Solar & Heliospheric Observatory (above). Launched in 1995, its 12 major scientific instruments are still studying the Sun's structure and provide regular data, allowing solar astronomers back on Earth to predict patterns of solar activity.

▼ LUNAR PHASES

The Moon, just like Earth, always has one side in darkness while the other side is bathed in light from the Sun. The amount of the Moon lit by the Sun that we can see from Earth alters each day. This amount is known as a phase. It varies from a new Moon, when the Moon is between the Sun and Earth with sunlight only falling on its far side, to a full Moon, when we can see all of its sunlit part because the Moon is on the opposite side of Earth from the Sun. A complete cycle of the Moon's phases takes 29.53 days.

▶ THE MOON

The Moon orbits Earth at an average distance of 238,900 miles (384,400 km). It has a diameter about one-quarter that of Earth. The Moon lacks an atmosphere, contains no surface water, and temperatures range from searing by day to frozen by night. Much of its surface is covered in a blanket of soil several meters thick and rising to 33 ft (10 m) in depth in some mountainous regions.

The Moon waxes as the phases grow larger, and wanes as they grow smaller

▼ TIDES

While Earth's gravitational pull ensures that the Moon stays in orbit around the planet, the Moon's own gravity has effects on Earth. Water in the planet's oceans is pulled toward the Moon. Its gravity creates two bulges in the water on either side of the planet. As Earth rotates on its axis, the bulges move around the planet, causing rises and falls in the ocean level. These are called tides.

Generally, there are two high tides each day

◀ LUNAR SURFACE ▶

As the Moon travels in its orbit around Earth, it also rotates on its axis. It takes as long to complete a full rotation as it does to circle Earth, which is why it always presents the same face to us. This near side of the Moon features many plains called maria, deep valleys called rills, and hundreds of impact craters. The largest, Bailly, is more than 180 miles (295 km) wide. The far side of the Moon was a mystery until space probes began photographing its surface in 1959.

ASTEROIDS, METEORITES, AND COMETS

The planets and their moons are not alone in the Solar System. There are many other bodies orbiting the Sun. Some, such as the millions of small meteoroids, are less than a meter across. Others, like the largest asteroids, Ceres, Pallas, and Vesta, can measure hundreds of miles in diameter, while the tail of a comet can extend millions of miles behind its nucleus. Many of the asteroids in the Solar System are believed to be the remains of a planet that failed to survive.

Trojan asteroids

Jupiter

Earth

Sun

Mars

Asteroid belt

Trojan asteroids

ASTEROIDS ▼

Asteroids are chunks of rock or rocky metals. More than 210,000 have been identified and more than 15,000 have been named, but only a handful have been studied up close by space probes. Vesta, the third-largest asteroid in the asteroid belt, is the one asteroid bright enough to see with the naked eye.

Eros asteroid is 21.5 miles (34.4 km) long

▲ THE ASTEROID BELT

About 90 percent of all asteroids are found in a broad belt between Mars and Jupiter, 154–392 million miles (248–598 million km) from the Sun. The vast majority of these asteroids are less than a mile across, but some are much larger. In 2009 and 2010, two asteroids in the belt—65 Cybele and 24 Themis—were found to have ice on their surface. There are also two groups of asteroids, called the Trojans, orbiting in the same path as Jupiter.

▲ METEORS

Meteors are small pieces of rock, dust, and metal that enter Earth's atmosphere. Most are fragments of asteroids, but some are small pieces of debris from Mars, the Moon, or comets. Most meteors burn up in the atmosphere in seconds, melting and forming streaks of light in the night sky known as falling or shooting stars.

A collection of meteors, called a shower, lights up part of the night sky

▼ COMETS

A comet consists of a solid nucleus surrounded by a cloud of dust and gas called the coma. The nucleus is often called a dirty snowball, and consists of frozen water, rock, metal, and carbon. As a comet approaches the Sun, heat evaporates or sublimates some of the ice into gas, increasing the size of the coma, which lengthens to become the comet's tail.

Comet Hale-Bopp could be viewed from Earth for 18 months (1995–97)

PERIODIC COMETS ▲

Comets have highly elliptical orbits around the Sun. Some take many thousands of years to complete an orbit. Much of what we know about comets comes from short-period comets such as Halley's Comet, which completes an orbit every 76 years.

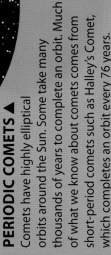
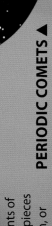
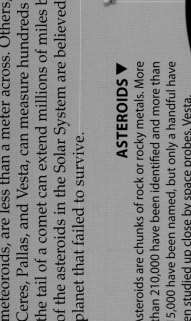

▶ DWARF PLANETS

In 2006, Pluto was relegated from one of the nine major Solar System planets to the status of dwarf planet. These are bodies that are basically spherical in shape and orbit the Sun and not another planet, but are not large enough for their gravitational pull to clear their orbital path of debris. Also classified as dwarf planets are Makemake, Eris, and Haumea, which lie inside the Kuiper Belt, and Ceres, the largest of the asteroids.

Pluto, as seen by the Hubble Space Telescope

IMPACT! ▶

When a meteorite or comet strikes Earth, it leaves an impact crater. Due to the high speed of impact, the resulting crater is often far larger than the body that crashed into the ground. Meteor Crater in Arizona (right) was formed around 50,000 years ago. It is 0.75 miles (1.2 km) wide, but was created by an asteroid that was only 100 ft (30 m) wide.

METEORITES ▼

Some larger meteors survive transit through the atmosphere and fall to Earth, where they are known as meteorites. Compared to meteors, meteorite occurrence is relatively rare, with around 400–900 impacts reported each year. Most surviving meteorites are fist-sized, but larger examples have been discovered. The biggest was found in Hoba West, Namibia, and weighed more than 60 tons.

SEEING INTO SPACE

Many ancient civilizations became expert stargazers, plotting the paths of bodies across the night sky by eye. The invention of optical telescopes in the 17th century made it possible to see more, such as the moons of Jupiter. Advances in the 20th century brought more powerful optical telescopes, observatories launched into space, and the collection and analysis of other electromagnetic waves from space, such as radio waves, gamma rays, X-rays, and infrared.

▶ REFLECTING AND REFRACTING

Optical telescopes capture visible light from space. They are either refracting or reflecting. The first telescopes were refractors, created by putting two eyeglass lenses in a tube, one in front of the other. Refractors use lenses to collect and bend light to create a magnified image. Lenses are hard to build to a large size and suffer from chromatic aberration, creating colored fringes around an image. Reflecting telescopes use large, extremely smooth mirrors instead. While your eye has an aperture, or opening, of up to 0.3 in (7 mm) to let in light, reflecting telescopes can have apertures measured in meters.

Angled secondary mirror directs to the eyepiece

Light enters reflecting telescope

Reflecting telescope

Eye

Concave main mirror bends light and sends it toward secondary mirror

Eye

Eyepiece lens magnifies image

Refracting telescope

Light focused through objective lens

Light gathered in by telescope aperture

Arecibo radio telescope's dish measures 1,015 ft (305 m) in diameter

▲ RADIO TELESCOPES

Radio waves from space can be gathered, amplified, and studied as electronic images. Radio astronomy began in 1932 with Karl Jansky's discovery of radio static coming from the Milky Way. Since that time, bigger radio dishes or arrays of a number of dishes linked together have discovered pulsars (see page 113), detected radio waves from quasars and exploding stars, and explored the cosmic microwave background radiation.

Chandra image of
the remains of an
exploded supernova

▶ INVESTIGATING OTHER WAVES

Electromagnetic waves, such as ultraviolet and
X-rays, are also collected by astronomical instruments
on the ground or in space. The Chandra Observatory was launched
into space in 1999 and is still collecting imagery from the remains of
exploded stars, and the gases around pulsars and black holes.

▼ INFRARED ASTRONOMY

This modified Boeing 747SP carries SOFIA, the largest
airborne observatory in the world. In 2010, SOFIA
began studying infrared sources from space. Many
objects in the Universe are too cool and faint to be
detected using visible light, but can be observed by
infrared telescopes. Infrared astronomy has revealed
many bodies previously unseen.

Aircraft houses an
8 ft (2.5 m) wide
infrared telescope.

▲ OBSERVATORIES

Telescopes and other electronic astronomy devices
are located in specially made observatories. Many
observatories are sited in isolated places away from the
light pollution generated by large cities, and in regions
with a dry climate with few clouds to obscure viewing.
The Mauna Kea Observatory in Hawaii is perched more
than 13,800 ft (4,200 m) above sea level.

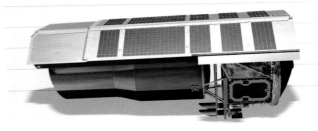

▶ THE HUBBLE

Launched in 1990 and
expected to operate until
2014, the Hubble Space
Telescope (HST) has helped
establish how the early
Universe worked by
peering back to galaxies
around 10 billion light-
years away. Its 8 ft (2.4 m)
diameter reflecting telescope
has studied newborn stars,
planets orbiting stars in other
galaxies, and comet impacts.

▲ SPACE OBSERVATORIES

X-rays and many other wavelengths of
electromagnetic radiation from space are
absorbed by Earth's atmosphere before
they reach the planet's surface. To gather
these rays, astronomers use satellites as
platforms to carry telescopes. Most of
these satellites orbit Earth. However, the
Spitzer Observatory, which investigates
infrared objects in space, was launched
in 2003 on a heliocentric orbit, traveling
around the Sun.

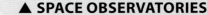

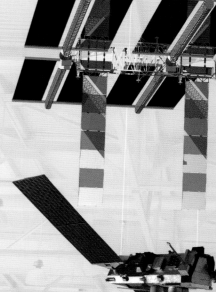

Solar array wing contains 32,800 solar cells

▶ SPACE STATIONS

Orbiting at an altitude of between 172 and 288 miles (278 and 460 km) above Earth's surface, the International Space Station (ISS) is the largest construction in space. Produced by the collaboration of 16 nations, the ISS was assembled in modules over the course of more than 50 spaceflights and 120 space walks. Since 2000, the 360 ft (110 m) long space station has provided a place for astronauts to work, live, and conduct a wide variety of long-term space-science experiments.

▲ LIFE IN SPACE

When astronauts leave Earth, they have to be orderly and methodical. Everyday tasks, such as eating, bathing, and sleeping, need to be managed carefully in a weightless environment. Inside the pressurized and air-conditioned cabins of the Space Shuttle and ISS, astronauts work in plain clothes and use footholds and straps to stay in one place.

▲ LIFTOFF

Rockets are chemical engines that mix fuel and oxygen, before burning this mixture in a combustion chamber. The hot gases accelerate out of the rocket's nozzle, while an equal and opposite force propels the rocket upward. The thrust produced by a rocket is enormous. Each of this Saturn V's five F1 engines generated 1.5 million lb (691,818 kg) of thrust, and in just 150 seconds they had propelled the rocket 42 miles (68 km) above Earth's surface.

SATELLITES ▶

Artificial satellites are launched to orbit Earth or other celestial bodies. Some satellites are in a geostationary orbit. This means that they orbit Earth at exactly the same speed as Earth turns, keeping the same position above the planet's surface. Geostationary satellites are used to predict the weather, for communications, and for navigation systems.

SPACE EXPLORATION

Sending people, probes, and scientific instruments into space has taught us much about the Solar System and Universe, as well as about our own planet. Manned space exploration is complex and costly, since large amounts of equipment, supplies, and life support systems are required. A method of returning astronauts to Earth safely is also needed. In contrast, unmanned space probes are expendable and can be sent on missions into space with no plans for their return.

▶ SPACE SUITS

For journeys to and from Earth and for space walks, specialized space suits are worn. NASA's EMU suit has 14 layers, with the outer layer able to repel small particles of rock that would rip through other materials. The suit contains a life support system. This keeps the suit pressurized and temperature-controlled, providing oxygen and transporting waste gases and liquids away.

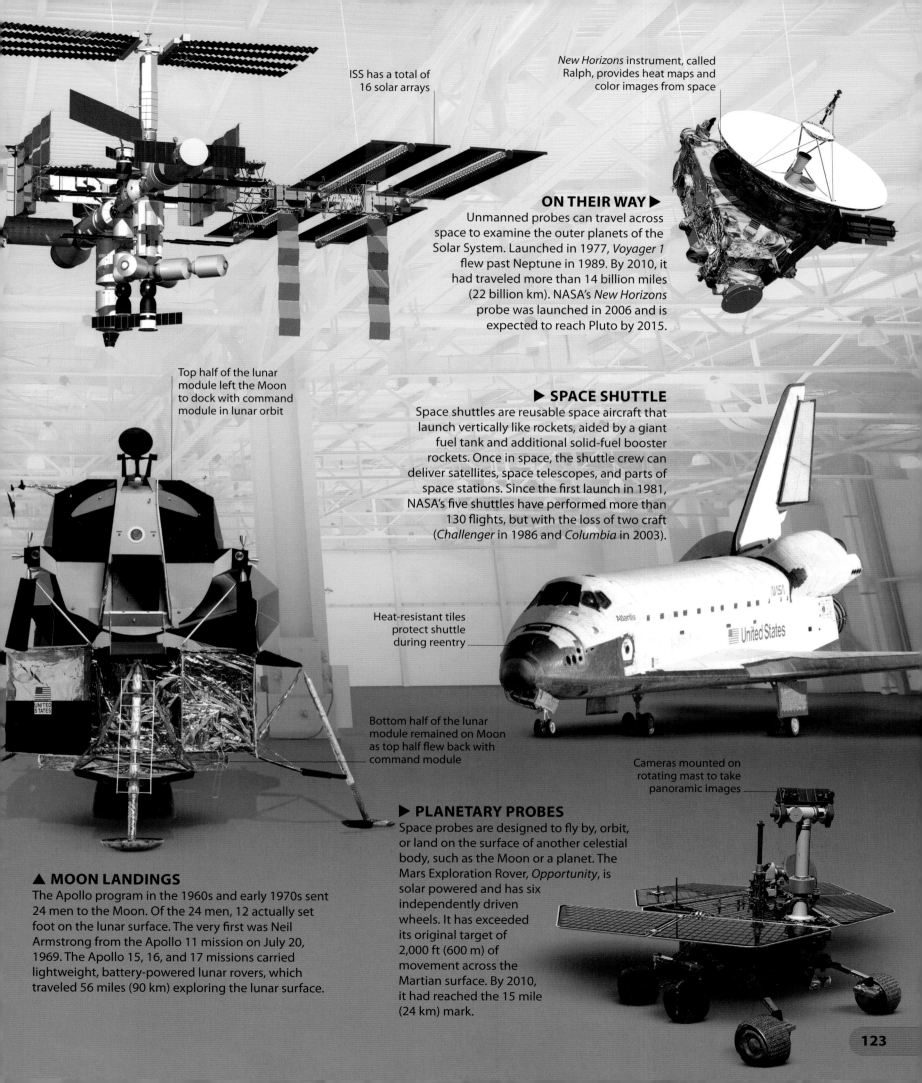

ISS has a total of
16 solar arrays

New Horizons instrument, called
Ralph, provides heat maps and
color images from space

ON THEIR WAY ▶

Unmanned probes can travel across
space to examine the outer planets of the
Solar System. Launched in 1977, *Voyager 1*
flew past Neptune in 1989. By 2010, it
had traveled more than 14 billion miles
(22 billion km). NASA's *New Horizons*
probe was launched in 2006 and is
expected to reach Pluto by 2015.

Top half of the lunar
module left the Moon
to dock with command
module in lunar orbit

▶ SPACE SHUTTLE

Space shuttles are reusable space aircraft that
launch vertically like rockets, aided by a giant
fuel tank and additional solid-fuel booster
rockets. Once in space, the shuttle crew can
deliver satellites, space telescopes, and parts of
space stations. Since the first launch in 1981,
NASA's five shuttles have performed more than
130 flights, but with the loss of two craft
(*Challenger* in 1986 and *Columbia* in 2003).

Heat-resistant tiles
protect shuttle
during reentry

Bottom half of the lunar
module remained on Moon
as top half flew back with
command module

Cameras mounted on
rotating mast to take
panoramic images

▲ MOON LANDINGS

The Apollo program in the 1960s and early 1970s sent
24 men to the Moon. Of the 24 men, 12 actually set
foot on the lunar surface. The very first was Neil
Armstrong from the Apollo 11 mission on July 20,
1969. The Apollo 15, 16, and 17 missions carried
lightweight, battery-powered lunar rovers, which
traveled 56 miles (90 km) exploring the lunar surface.

▶ PLANETARY PROBES

Space probes are designed to fly by, orbit,
or land on the surface of another celestial
body, such as the Moon or a planet. The
Mars Exploration Rover, *Opportunity*, is
solar powered and has six
independently driven
wheels. It has exceeded
its original target of
2,000 ft (600 m) of
movement across the
Martian surface. By 2010,
it had reached the 15 mile
(24 km) mark.

123

Glossary

ACID RAIN
Rain and snow that contains poisonous or harmful chemicals, such as sulfur dioxide, which are created by the burning of fossil fuels.

AMPHIBIANS
Creatures, such as frogs and toads, that are able to live on land or in water.

ANTENNA
A long sensory structure found on creatures such as insects.

ARTERY
A thick-walled blood vessel that carries blood away from an animal's heart.

ATMOSPHERE
The layer of gases that surrounds a moon, planet, or star.

ATOM
The smallest particle of a chemical element.

BACTERIA
Microscopic single-celled life forms. Bacteria are the most abundant living things on Earth.

BIG BANG
A massive event from which scientists believe the Universe expanded and formed about 13.7 billion years ago.

CARBON DIOXIDE
A gas that is found in the atmosphere and is a waste product of energy release in cells.

CELL
A tiny unit of living matter. Cells are the building blocks of all living things.

CENTRAL NERVOUS SYSTEM
The control center of the nervous system that consists of the brain and the spinal cord.

CHLOROPHYLL
The green-colored chemical that traps the sunlight energy plants use to make their food.

CHROMOSOME
A threadlike structure in a cell's nucleus. Chromosomes are made of DNA and contain genes.

COMET
A small body made of ice, dust, and rock particles that orbits the Sun and can grow a large tail when nearing the Sun.

COMPOUND
A substance containing two or more elements formed by a chemical reaction that bonds their atoms together.

COMPOUND EYE
A type of eye, found in insects and crustaceans, made up of many smaller units.

CONDENSE
To change from a gas to a liquid.

CONVECTION
The transfer of heat by movement—for example, when warm gas rises and cooler gas sinks.

CRUSTACEAN
A creature with a hard-shelled body, jointed legs, and two pairs of antennae.

DEFORESTATION
The cutting down of large numbers of trees for fuel or timber, or to clear the land for settlements or farming.

DENSITY
A measure of how tightly the mass of an object is packed into its volume.

DEOXYRIBONUCLEIC ACID (DNA)
The long molecules found in a cell nucleus that contain the coded instructions to build and operate a cell.

DIGESTION
The breaking down of food so that it can be absorbed and used by the body.

EARTHQUAKE
A large, sudden movement of Earth's crust.

ECOSYSTEM
A community of interacting living organisms and the environment.

ECTOTHERMIC
Describes an animal whose internal body temperature varies with its surroundings.

ELECTROMAGNETIC RADIATION
A range of energy waves that travel through space and include gamma rays, ultraviolet, infrared, visible light, and radio waves.

ELEMENT
One of just over 100 different types of atoms, such as gold, hydrogen, iron, and silicon, which form all substances.

ELLIPTICAL
Shaped like an ellipse—an elongated circle or sphere.

ENDOTHERMIC
Describes an animal whose internal body temperature remains the same. Also refers to a reaction that takes in energy from its surroundings.

ENZYME
A substance that controls the rate of chemical reactions, including the breakdown of food molecules during digestion.

EQUATOR
The imaginary line drawn around the center of the Earth an equal distance from the North and South Poles.

EROSION
The wearing away and transportation of rock through natural forces, such as wind or flowing water.

EVAPORATION
The process by which a liquid changes into a gas. The warming of the air by the Sun causes water to evaporate and change into water vapor.

EVOLUTION
The process by which species change over many generations and long periods of time to give rise to new species.

EXOPLANET
A planet that orbits around a star other than our Sun.

FAULT
A fracture or crack in Earth's crust where blocks of rock slip past each other.

FOOD CHAIN
The links between different animals that feed on plants and each other. Food chains show how energy is passed up through the chain.

FOSSIL FUEL
A type of fuel, such as coal, gas, or oil, that formed underground over millions of years from the remains of plants and animals.

FRICTION
The resistance created by the rubbing of one moving object or material against another object or material.

FUNGI
A group of living organisms that includes mushrooms.

GALAXY
An enormous grouping of stars, planets, gases, and dust that is held together by gravity.

GENE
One of the instructions stored inside cells required to build and operate an organism's body. Genes are passed on from parents to their offspring.

GLACIER
A mass of ice formed from compacted snow that may flow slowly downhill.

GRAVITY
A force of attraction between objects found throughout the Universe. The greater an object's mass, the greater its gravitational pull.

HABITAT
The natural home of a species of animal or other living organism.

HEMISPHERE
One of the halves of Earth created by the equator.

HORMONE
A substance released by a gland into the bloodstream that acts as a chemical messenger. Some hormones help control certain body processes, such as the rate of body growth.

IGNEOUS ROCK
A rock formed from the cooling and hardening of hot liquid magma or lava.

INSECT
A hard-shelled creature with a three-part body, six legs, and usually two pairs of wings.

INVERTEBRATE
An animal without a backbone, such as an insect.

JOINT
A part of the skeleton where two or more bones meet, for example the elbow.

KERATIN
A tough, waterproof substance found in nails, hair, and the outer layers of skin.

LAVA
Magma that reaches Earth's surface through a volcanic vent or fissure.

LIGHT-YEAR
A unit of distance equal to the distance light travels through space in one year. One light-year is equal to 5.9 trillion miles (9.5 trillion km).

MAGMA
Hot liquid rock that lies beneath Earth's surface.

MAMMAL
An endothermic vertebrate, such as a dog or horse, that has fur or hair and feeds its young with milk.

MANTLE
The rocky middle layer of the Earth that lies between its core and outer crust.

METAMORPHIC ROCK
A type of rock formed when igneous or sedimentary rock is altered by great heat or pressure, or both.

METEOR
A short-lived streak of light, which is produced by a small piece of rocky material from space traveling through Earth's upper atmosphere.

METEORITE
A piece of rock or metal that lands on the surface of a planet or moon.

MOLECULE
A group of atoms that are bonded together. For example, oxygen and hydrogen atoms are bonded together in a water molecule.

NERVE
A bundle of long, specialized cells that relay signals rapidly from one part of the body to another.

NUCLEAR FISSION
The splitting of the nuclei of atoms to generate enormous energy for use in power plants or weapons.

NUCLEAR FUSION
The fusing, or combining, of atoms of two elements to create a heavier element.

ORBIT
The path that a natural body, such as a moon, or an artificial object, such as a space probe, makes around a larger body.

ORE
A type of mineral that contains useful metals, such as iron, that can be extracted.

ORGANISM
An individual form of life, such as a single-celled bacterium, an animal, or a plant.

PHOTOSYNTHESIS
The process by which plants use energy from sunlight to produce food.

PLATE TECTONICS
The process in which the large plates that form Earth's crust are constantly moving together or apart.

POLLUTION
Waste products or heat that damage the environment in some way.

PRECIPITATION
Any form of water, such as rain, snow, sleet, or hail, that falls from the atmosphere to the surface of the Earth.

PRESSURE
The force felt when something presses against a surface.

PREY
An animal that is killed and eaten by another animal, the predator.

PRODUCER
An organism, such as a plant, that makes its own food using sunlight energy and provides nutrients and energy to any animals that eat it.

PROTOSTAR
A very young star in its early stages of formation before nuclear reactions begin in its core.

RADIATION
Energy traveling as electromagnetic waves, such as infrared or visible light.

RESERVOIR
A natural or artificial store of liquid, usually water.

RESPIRATION
A chemical process in which food is broken down to release energy.

SEDIMENT
A solid that settles at the bottom of a liquid.

SEDIMENTARY ROCK
A type of rock formed from sediment that is compressed over time to form a solid.

SOLUBLE
Capable of being dissolved.

SPECIES
A set of organisms that can be grouped together due to their similarity and their potential ability to breed with each other.

SPECTRUM
The rainbow band of colors that is produced when light is split.

STEM CELL
An unspecialized cell that divides repeatedly, giving rise to specialized cells, such as nerve cells or muscle cells.

STRATA
Layers of sedimentary rock.

SUPERNOVA
A star that explodes and leaves a remnant behind that may become a black hole, pulsar, or neutron star. The plural of supernova is supernovae.

SYSTEM
A set of linked organs inside an animal's body, such as the nervous system or digestive system, which carries out a specific set of functions.

TOXIC
Poisonous or harmful.

TRIBUTARIES
Streams or small rivers that flow into larger rivers.

TRILLION
One million million (one followed by 12 zeros).

VEIN
A blood vessel that carries blood from an animal's tissues back to its heart.

VERTEBRATE
An animal that has a backbone. Fish, mammals, amphibians, birds, and reptiles are all vertebrate animals.

VISCOUS
Refers to a liquid and how slowly it runs.

VOLUME
The amount of space an object occupies.

WATER CYCLE
The continual flow of Earth's water from the atmosphere to Earth and back.

WAVELENGTH
The distance between the peaks or troughs in waves of energy.

WEATHERING
The gradual breaking down of rocks and minerals into sand and soil.

Index

Bold page numbers refer to
main entries

A

AC (alternating current) 105
acceleration 89
acid rain 62
acids 78–79
adaptation 14, 21
air pollution 62, 63
air resistance 87
alimentary canal 35
alkalis 68, 78
alloys 76, 80, 81
amphibians 18–19
amplitude 94
Andromeda Galaxy 109, 110, 111
ants 17
Apollo program 123
arachnids 16–17
Archaeopteryx 14
arteries 32, 33
asteroid belt 114, 118–19
astronomy 116, 120–21
atmosphere 45, 58, 63, 114
atoms 66–67, 68, 100, 108
auroras 71
axle 90
aye-aye 14

B

bacteria 8, 9, 27, 35, 45
bases 78–79
batteries 79, 104, 105
beak 21
bees 16, 17, 27
beetles 17
Big Bang 108
Big Crunch 109
binary stars 112
birds 14, 20–21
bitumen 80
black dwarf 113
black hole 113
blood 32–33
body repair 38–39
bones 20, 22, 24
    broken 38
    human skeleton 30–31
bony fish 22
brain 36–37
breathing 19, 22, 32–33
brown dwarf 112
butterflies 16

C

calories 96
capillaries 33
carbon dioxide 8, 33, 67
carnivores 8, 11
cartilage 22, 31
catalysts 75
cells 9, 28, 35, 38, 40
cephalopods 23
Ceres 114, 118, 119
Chandra Observatory 121
chemical energy 85

chemical reaction 74–75, 76, 98
chewing 35
chlorophyll 10, 11
chromatography 77
chromosomes 40
circuit breakers 104
circuit diagrams 101
circulatory system 32–33
climate change 63
cloning 41
clouds 57, 58, 59
cnidarians 23
coastal erosion 53
cold-blooded animals 18
color 93, 99
combustion 98
comets 118–19
commensalism 27
compounds 74, 76–77
condensation 70
conduction 79, 97, 101
continental drift 44, 46
contraction 96
convection 97
copper sulfate 79
coral 6, 23, 63
cosmology 108
crane 91
crustaceans 23
current 100

D

dark energy 109
dark matter 109
DC (direct current) 105
decibel 94
decomposers 27
deforestation 63
Deimos 115
density 72
desertification 63
digestive system 34–35
diseases 33, 62
distillation 77, 80
DNA 40, 41
dodo 15
drought 57

E

eagles 8, 20, 21
Earth 42–63, 86, 114
    crust 44, 45, 46, 48, 50
    life 8–9, 44, 45
    magnetic field 103, 116
    origins 44–45
    structure 45
earthquakes 48–49
echinoderms 23
echoes 95
ecosystems 26–27
eggs 18, 19, 20, 21, 24
elasticity 72, 85
electrical conductivity 73
electrical energy 84, 99
electric current 100
electricity 79, 100–101
    generation of 61, 104
    using 104–105

electric light 99
electric motor 103
electric vehicles 105
electrolysis 104
electromagnetic induction 105
electromagnetic spectrum
    92–93, 98, 120, 121
electromagnetism 102, 103
electroplating 105
elements 50, 66
    periodic table 68–69
endangered species 15
endocrine system 28
energy 61, 84–85, 92, 96, 116
    food 8, 26
Eris 115, 119
erosion 52–53
esophagus 35
estivation 19
Etna, Mount 48, 49
evaporation 70, 77
evolution 14–15, 24
exoskeleton 16
expansion 96
extinction 14–15, 49, 63
eyes 16, 36

F

farming 61
faults 46–47, 48
feathers 14, 20
fish 22
fishing 61
flammability 73
flexibility 72
flies 16
flight 20, 21
floods 57
flowers 8, 12, 27
fog 58
food 8, 9, 21, 84, 85
    digestion 34–35
food chains 26
forces 82, 86–87, 88
forests 61, 63
fossil fuels 61, 62
fossils 14, 54–55
fractures 38
freezing 71
frequency 92, 94
friction 86
frogs 19, 26
fruits 12
fulcrum 91
fungi 8, 27
fur 25
fuses 104

G

galaxies 108, 109, 110–11
galvanizing 74
gamma rays 92, 120
Ganymede 115
gases 69, 71
gears 90
generator 105
genetics 40–41
geological time 54
germination 12
glaciation 52
glands 28
glass 81, 98
gravity 86, 117
growth 9

H

habitats 26
hailstones 58
hair 25
hardness 72
hearing 37
heart 32, 31, 33
heat 84, 96–97
Hemiptera 17
herbivores 8
hormones 28, 29, 32
hot springs 45
Hubble Space Telescope 121
human body 28–29
human genome project 41
humidity 58
hurricanes 59
hydroelectric power 61

I

ice caps 56, 63
igneous rocks 50
impact craters 119
inclined plane 90
inertia 89
infrared 93, 96, 120, 121
inheritance 40
insects 16–17, 26
insulators 25, 73, 97, 100
International Space Station 122
intestines 35
invertebrates 16
Io 115
isotopes 66

J K

Jansky, Karl 120
jaw 25
joints 31, 39
Jupiter 115
karst 52
kinetic energy 84
Kuiper belt 115

L

lasers 98
lava 48, 49
leaves 10, 11, 63
legumes 13
lenses 99, 120
levers 91
life 8–9, 44, 45, 56, 116
    extraterrestrial 109
    underwater 22–23
light 92, 93, 98–99
light bulbs 99
lightning 59, 100
light years 108
liquids 70
live young 18, 24
Local Group 111
loudspeaker 95, 102
lubrication 86
lungs 32, 33

M

machines, simple 90–91
maglev train 102
magnetic fields 103
magnetism 102–103
magnitude 111

mammals 22, **24–25**
marine life **22–23**, 25
Mars 114, 115
marsupials 24
mass extinction 15
materials science **80–81**
matter 66
    properties of **72–73**
    states of **70–71**
Mendeleev, Dmitri 68
Mercury 114
melting 71
metals 61, 73, 74, 97
    alloys 76, 80, 81
    periodic table 68, 69
metamorphic rocks 51
metamorphosis 16
meteorites **118–19**
meteors 118
methane 67
microphone 95
microwaves 93
Milky Way 110, 120
minerals 50, 61
mining 61
mixtures **76–77**
molecules 66, 67
mollusks 23
momentum 89
monotremes 24
Moon 86, **116–17**
    landings 123
    phases of 117
moons 115
motion **88–89**
motor, electric 103
mountains 46, 47
movement 8, 31, 88
muscles 20, 28, **30–31**
musical instruments 94
mutualism 27

N

nanotechnology 81
natural resources **61–62**
natural selection 14
nebulae 106, 112
Neptune 114
nervous system 28, 36, 100
nests 18, 21
neutron stars 113
Newton, Sir Isaac 88, 89
nuclear fission 67, 85, 112, 116
nuclear fusion 85

O

observatories 116, 120, 121
oceans 44, 46, 53, 56, 61
    life **22–23**
    tides 117
oil, crude 80
omnivores 8
ores 61
organs 28, 29, 31
Orion Nebula 106
Orthoptera 17
oxygen 8, 22, 32, 33, 44, 66

P

pancreas 29
parasitism 27
parenting 24
periodic table **68–69**

petroleum 80
pH scale 78
Phobos 115
photons 98
photosynthesis 8, 10, 12, 27
phototropism 9
pitch 94
pivot 89
planetary nebulae 113
planetary probes 123
planets 114–15
    dwarf 115, 119
plankton 22
plants 8, 9, 26
    reproduction **12–13**
    structure **10–11**
plasma 71
plasticity 73
plastics 80
plates, Earth's **46–47**, 48
Pluto 115, 119
pollination 12, 17
pollution 62
polymers 76
population growth 62
potential energy 84
power plant 61, 62, 104
pressure 87
propane 67
proprioception 37
prostheses 39
protists 8
protostars 112
pulleys 91
pulsars 113, 120

R

radiation 96
radio telescope 120
radio waves 93, 120
rain 57
rainbow 93
ramp 90
reaction force 89
recycling 81
red giant 112
reflection 99
refraction 98
renewable energy 61
reproduction 9
    plants **12–13**
reptiles **18–19**
resistance 101
resonance 95
respiration 8
responsiveness 9
rivers 51, 53, 56, 61
rockets 122
rocks 42, **50–51**, 61
    erosion **52–53**
    strata **54–55**
Röntgen, Wilhelm Conrad 92
roots 10, 11

S

saliva 35
salts **78–79**
Santorini 49
saponification 79
satellites 122
Saturn 115
scissors 91
scorpions 17
screwdriver 90

sedimentary rock 50, 51, 54
seeds 12, 13
seesaw 91
semiconductors 101
senses 25, 29, **36–37**
Shape Memory Alloys 81
shells 19, 23
shooting stars 118
shovel 91
sight 36
skeleton 20, 22, 24
    human **30–31**
skin 19, 29, 36, 38
smell 37
snakes 18, 19, 26
snow 58
soap 79
sodium bicarbonate 79
SOHO probe 116
soil 27, **50–51**
solar flare 116
Solar System 44, 110, **114–15**
solar wind 116
solids 71
solubility 73
solutions 76
sound 37, 84, **94–95**
space 106–123
space exploration **122–23**
space observatories 116, 121
space probes 116, 122, 123
Space Shuttle 122, 123
space stations 122
space suits 122
species 8
speed 89
    of sound 94
spiders 17
Spitzer Observatory 121
sponges 23
spores 13
stars **110–11**
    life and death **112–13**
static electricity 100
stomach 35
storms 59, 114
strata **54–55**
subatomic particles 64
sulfur 66
sulfuric acid 78
Sun 85, 96, 98, **116–17**
    Solar System 44, 110, **114–15**
sunspots 116
supergiant 112
supernova 113
swallowing 35
swim bladder 22
synovial joints 31

T

taste 37
teeth 25, 35
telescopes **120–21**
thermal conductivity 73
thermometer 96
thunder 59
tides 117
tissue 28
toads 19, 27
tongue 35
touch 29, 36
transformer 105
transparency 98
transpiration 11
transplants 39

Triton 115
tsunamis 48
turning force 89

U V

ultrasound 94
ultraviolet rays 93, 121
Universe **108–109**
urinary system 29
vegetative reproduction 13
veins 32, 33
velocity 89
Venus 114
Venus flytrap 11
vertebrates 18, 20, 24
Vesta 118
vestigial structures 15
vibration 94, 95
vinegar 78
volcanoes **48–49**

W X

warm-blooded animals 25
wasps 17
waste disposal 63
water 13, **56–57**, 61, 70, 73
    erosion 53
    life in **22–23**
    molecule 67, 76
    pollution 62, 63
water cycle 56
waterfalls 53
wavelength 92, 99
weather **58–59**, 63
weathering **52–53**
weightlessness 122
wetlands 57
wheat 61
wheel 90
wheelbarrow 91
white dwarf 113
wind 13, 53, 59, 61, 114
wings 16, 17, 20
wounds, healing 38
X-rays 92, 120, 121

Acknowledgments

DK would like to thank:
Chris Bernstein for preparing the index.

Picture Credits
The publisher would like to thank the following for their kind permission to reproduce their photographs:

(Key: a-above; b-below/bottom; c-center; l-left; r-right; t-top)

4 Corbis: (tl); Science Faction/Dan McCoy (crb). **Getty Images:** Riser/Jack Dykinga (tr). **5 Corbis:** Lester Lefkowitz (tl). **NASA:** ESA, M. Robberto (Space Telescope Science Institute/ESA) and the Hubble Space Telescope Orion Treasury Project Team (tr). **6-7 Corbis. 8 Corbis:** George H.H. Huey (cr); Frank Lane Picture Agency (cl). **Getty Images:** Discovery Channel Images/Jeff Foott (bc); Workbook Stock/Ed Morris (c); Visuals Unlimited (bl). **9 Corbis:** Visuals Unlimited/Dr. Richard Kessel & Dr. Gene Shih (tc) (tl). **iStockphoto.com:** (br). **10 Corbis:** David Aubrey (c); Visuals Unlimited/Biodisc (tr). **Dreamstime.com:** Graeme Dawes (br) (Background Daisies). **iStockphoto.com:** (Background Window). **11 Corbis:** AgStock Images (c); Visuals Unlimited/Dr. Stanley Flegler (bl). **Getty Images:** CMSP/J.L. Carson (tl); GAP Photos/Maxine Adcock (Background); Photodisc/Don Farrall (br). **iStockphoto.com:** Wojtek Kryczka (bl/Wooden Board). **12 Getty Images:** Photodisc/Martin Ruegner (tl). **12-13 Getty Images:** Photographer's Choice/Cornelia Doerr (b/Sunflowers). **13 Corbis:** Design Pics/John Short (c); Ecoscene/Sally A. Morgan (br); Visuals Unlimited/Dr. Richard Kessel & Dr. Gene Shih (bl). **Dorling Kindersley:** Geoff Brightling/Peter Minister (Modelmaker) (cl). **14 Corbis:** Ecoscene/Sally A. Morgan (ca); Frans Lanting (cb); Science Faction/Steven Kazlowski (ca). **14-15 iStockphoto.com:** (Background Stamps); Michael Cavén (Stamp Templates 2); Matt Knannlein (Franking Marks); David Mingay (Stamp Templates). **15 Corbis:** Tom Brakefield (bl); JAI/Nigel Pavitt (bc); Reuters/Victor Fraile (br); Visuals Unlimited (tc). **Getty Images:** Archive Photos (c); Photographer's Choice/Colin Anderson (tr). **16 Dorling Kindersley:** Courtesy of the Natural History Museum, London/Frank Greenaway (tr/Moth) (cl). **Getty Images:** Photographer's Choice/Gail Shumway (tl). **iStockphoto.com:** Martin Lladó (tr/Bulb); Marcin Pasko (bl/Parchment). **17 iStockphoto.com:** Matthew Cole (c); Aleksander Trankov (cr). **18 Dreamstime.com:** David Davis (tl); Eric Isselée (b). **Getty Images:** The Image Bank/Roger de la Harpe (cb/Crocodile Eggs). **iStockphoto.com:** Nieves Mares Pagán (cb/Background Fern). **18-19 Getty Images:** The Image Bank/Anup Shah (tc). **iStockphoto.com:** Olena Pantiukh (b/Sand). **19 Corbis:** Frank Lane Picture Agency/Chris Mattison (ca). **Getty Images:** Gallo Images/Martin Harvey (tc); Rodger Jackman (br). **20 Alamy Images:** blickwinkel (bl). **Corbis:** Visuals Unlimited/Dennis Kunkel Microscopy, Inc (crb). **Dorling Kindersley:** Courtesy of the Booth Museum of Natural History, Brighton/Alex Wilson (l). **21 Corbis:** DPA/Patrick Pleul (cl). **Dorling Kindersley:** Courtesy of the Natural History Museum, London/Peter Chadwick (l/Falling Feathers). **22 Corbis:** Visuals Unlimited (tc). **Dorling Kindersley:** Courtesy of the Natural History Museum, London/Dave King (br). **Getty Images:** Workbook Stock/Na Gen Imaging (cr). **iStockphoto.com:** Hals Van IJzendoorn (Background). **23 Corbis:** Brandon D. Cole (c/Sponge). **Dorling Kindersley:** Bill Noll (Spotted Background). **24 Corbis:** DPA/Carmen Jaspersen (tr). **Getty Images:** Gallo Images/Nigel Dennis (c); The Image Bank/Winfried Wisniewski (cr); Newspix (bl). **iStockphoto.com:** Andrew Johnson (cr). **24-25 iStockphoto.com:** Kjell Brynildsen (Wooden Background); Michel de Nijs (b). **25 Corbis:** Paul Souders (tl); Visuals Unlimited (cb). **Getty Images:** The Image Bank/James Warwick (tr). **iStockphoto.com:** Franco Deriu (c); Ermin Gutenberger (br). **Photolibrary:** Michael Habicht (br/Camera Screen). **26 Corbis:** All Canada Photos/Wayne Lynch (tr). **iStockphoto.com:** Dave White (tr/Frame); John Woodworth (b/Clock & Vase). **26-27 iStockphoto.com:** Spiderstock (b/Mantelpiece). **27 Corbis:** Nathan Griffiths (clb); Frans Lanting (cla). **Dorling Kindersley:** Judith Miller/Sloan's (br/Frame). **Getty Images:** Stockfood Creative/Wolfgang Feiler (tc); Tetra Images (clb/Picture Holder); Ian Waldie (br). **iStockphoto.com:** (c/Frame); Jon Schulte (cr/Frame). **28 Dorling Kindersley:** Donks Models/Geoff Dann (cla); Old Operating Theatre Museum, London/Steve Gorton (tr). **28-29 Getty Images:** Digital Vision/Andersen Ross (Background). **29 Dorling Kindersley:** Denoyer-Geppert - modelmaker/Geoff Brightling (cl) (bl); Chris Reynolds and the BBC Team - modelmakers/Geoff Brightling (cr). **30 Dorling Kindersley:** ESPL - modelmaker/Geoff Brightling (r). **iStockphoto.com:** Alexander Ivanov (bl). **30-31 iStockphoto.com:** (Computer). **31 Corbis:** Visuals Unlimited (cr). **Getty Images:** 3D4Medical.com (l). **iStockphoto.com:** Feng Yu (b). **32 Corbis:** Micro Discovery (tr). **Getty Images:** Comstock Images (bl). **32-33 Getty Images:** Photographer's Choice/Peter Dazeley (b/Background Instruments). **33 MedicalRF.com** (bc); Randy (bl). **Getty Images:** George Doyle & Ciaran Griffin (tr); Stone+/Roy Ritchie (tl/Background). **34 Corbis:** Visuals Unlimited/Dennis Kunkel Microscopy, Inc (br/Intestine). **Getty Images:** Peter Hince (cra/Sweetcorn). **iStockphoto.com:** (clb/Truck); Jon Patton (t/Truck) (cra/Truck); Tomasz Pietryszek (cla/Truck). **34-35 Getty Images:** Brand X Pictures/Jetta Productions (Background Overpass).

35 Corbis: Visuals Unlimited/Dennis Kunkel Microscopy, Inc (br/Bacteria). **iStockphoto.com:** Tomasz Pietryszek (crb). **36 Dorling Kindersley:** Denoyer-Geppert - modelmaker/Geoff Brightling (crb). **36-37 iStockphoto.com:** Paolo de Santis (Background). **37 Corbis:** Visuals Unlimited/Dennis Kunkel Microscopy, Inc (tr). **Dorling Kindersley:** Denoyer-Geppert - modelmaker/Geoff Brightling (bl). **Getty Images:** AFP/Stringer (cr). **38 Corbis:** Bettmann (tl); MedicalRF.com (cla); Science Photo Library/Miriam Maslo (tr/X-Ray); Xinhua Press/Chen Xiaowei (b). **Getty Images:** Stone/Alan Thornton (b/Leg in Plaster); Taxi/Dana Neely (tr/Lightbox). **iStockphoto.com:** Andrzej Tokarski (c). **40 Corbis:** Beau Lark (c). **Getty Images:** Workbook Stock/Steven Puetzer (cl). **40-41 iStockphoto.com:** (Fridge); Glen Coventry (Magnetic Numbers). **41 Corbis:** (tr); SABA/Najlah Feanny (c). **Getty Images:** Photographer's Choice/Peter Dazeley (bc). **42-43 Getty Images:** Riser/Jack Dykinga. **44 iStockphoto.com:** Andrew Furlong Photography (Cupcakes); Maya Kovacheva (c). **44-45 iStockphoto.com:** (c/Book); Luis Albuquerque (Wooden Background). **45 Corbis:** Visuals Unlimited/Dr. Henry Aldrich (cr/Cyanobacteria). **Dorling Kindersley:** Satellite Imagemap © 1996-2003 Planetary Visions (cr). **Getty Images:** Koichi Kamoshida (bc); StockFood Creative/Barbara Bonisolli (tr/Flour). **iStockphoto.com:** Konstantin Kirillov (b/Tea Towels); Stepan Popov (cr). **46 Corbis:** Arctic-Images (cb/Lava). **46-47 Getty Images:** Photographer's Choice (Floor); Photonica/Nichola Evans (Dustpan and Shards). **iStockphoto.com:** Павел Игнатов (Plates). **47 Corbis:** Lloyd Cluff (tl/San Andreas); Frank Lukasseck (tr/Andes). **48 Corbis:** Roger Ressmeyer (bl). **Dorling Kindersley:** Peter Griffiths - modelmaker/Matthew Ward (cra). **Getty Images:** AFP/Juan Barreto (cl); Stone/Jorg Greuel (r/Stacked DVDs) (cra/DVD Cover). **iStockphoto.com:** Nicolas Hansen (cl/DVD Cover). **48-49 Getty Images:** Riser/Steven Puetzer (Shelves). **iStockphoto.com:** Nicolas Hansen (DVD). **49 Corbis:** Douglas Peebles (bc). **Dorling Kindersley:** Atlantic Digital (tc). **Getty Images:** AFP/Antonov Mladen (br); Photographer's Choice/VolcanoDiscovery/Tom Pfeiffer (cr) (clb); Planet Observer/Universal Images Group (c). **iStockphoto.com:** Nicolas Hansen (bc/DVD Cover). **50 Dorling Kindersley:** Donks Models - modelmaker/Andy Crawford (cr/Rock Cycle). **Dreamstime.com:** (cr/Book). **Getty Images:** Jamie Grill (Background). **51 Dorling Kindersley:** Courtesy of the Natural History Museum, London/Colin Keates (tl); Oxford University Museum of Natural History/Neil Fletcher (tr). **iStockphoto.com:** Milan Brunclik (c); Christopher Hudson (Background). **NASA:** GSFC/METI/ERSDAC/JAROS, and U.S./Japan ASTER Science Team (cl). **52 Corbis:** Hal Beral (br); Frans Lanting (tr); Visuals Unlimited/Gerald & Buff Corsi (tc) (c). **52-53 Getty Images:** Riser/Stuart Westmorland (Background). **53 Corbis:** Yann Arthus-Bertrand (bl); Lowell Georgia (br); Momatiuk - Eastcott (c). **Getty Images:** Robert Harding World Imagery/James Hager (tc). **54 Corbis:** Richard Hamilton Smith (cl); Visuals Unlimited (bl). **Dorling Kindersley:** Courtesy of Dinosaur State Park, Connecticut/Ed Homonylo (bc). **iStockphoto.com:** Ola Dusegård (Blinds). **55 Alamy Images:** David R. Frazier Photolibrary, Inc (bl). **Corbis:** All Canada Photos/Thomas Kitchin & Victoria Hurst (c/View). **Dorling Kindersley:** Courtesy of the Natural History Museum, London/Colin Keates (br). **iStockphoto.com:** Red Cover/Kim Sayer (c/Frame). **iStockphoto.com:** (bl/Frame). **56 Corbis:** Reuters/Bob Strong (tr/Ice Cap). **Getty Images:** Taxi/Richard H. Johnston (cl/Wave). **iStockphoto.com:** Greg Nicholas (tr/Bottle); Kais Tolmats (l/Lilos); Андрей Данилович (tl/Surf). **56-57 iStockphoto.com:** Yosef Galanti (Background Sand). **57 Corbis:** Bettmann (bl/Floods); Image Source (tr/Drought); JAI/Nigel Pavitt (cr/Wetlands). **Getty Images:** AFP/Karen Bleier (tl/Cloud) (cb/Sunglasses). **iStockphoto.com:** (cl/Stick); Zyuzin Andriy (br/Pen); Don Bayley (tr/Sun Screen); Dmitry Mordvintsev (cr/Book). **58 Corbis:** Gary W. Carter (cr/Fog); Dean Conger (bl/Rain); Eric Nguyen (bc/Hail). **Getty Images:** Mike Kemp (cr/Shirt); Pamela Moore (cl/Tea Towel). **58-59 Getty Images:** amana images/Doable (c/Clothes); UVimages (Background Sky). **59 Corbis:** EPA/Craig Connor (cl/Wind); Jim Reed Photography (tc/Thunderstorm). **Getty Images:** Comstock (ca/Lightning); The Image Bank/Microzoa (tc/Pants); Photographer's Choice/Mitchell Funk (cl/Snow). **NASA:** (tr/Hurricane). **60 Corbis:** Jason Hawkes (bl/Mine); Lester Lefkowitz (br/Dam); Benjamin Rondel (c/Logging); Science Faction/Natalie Fobes (cl/Fishing). **Getty Images:** All Canada Photos/Dave Reede (c/Farming); Digital Vision/Joe Sohm (cr/Quarry); Riser/Nicolas Russell (bc/Oil Rig). **iStockphoto.com:** Ingus Evertovskis (b/Packaging); Alex van de Hoef (c/Packaging); Dmitry Naumov (c/Packaging). **60-61 iStockphoto.com:** Ethan Myerson (Vending Machine). **61 Getty Images:** Lonely Planet Images/Paul Kennedy (c/Wind Farm). **iStockphoto.com:** studioaraminta (cb/Acid Rain); Will & Deni McIntyre (cb/Acid Rain). **62 Corbis:** Universal Images Group (tl); Workbook Stock/Stephane Godin (cr/Pollution). **iStockphoto.com:** (cb/Junk); dutch icon (tl/Hazard Signs); Cheryl Savala (cr/Junk). **62-63 iStockphoto.com:** Loic Bernard (Sewage Pipe). **63 Corbis:** Reuters/Rickey Rogers (tc/Logging). **Getty Images:** AFP/Ove Hoegh-Guidberg (br/Coral); Gallo Images/Danita Delimont (b/Sign); The Image Bank/Remi Benali (c/Desertification); Stone/Stephen Wilkes (cl/Landfill). **iStockphoto.com:** (tc/Junk); Claudio Arnese (bl/Tyre); Seb Crocker (cl/Junk); Yong

Hian Lim (br/Junk). **64-65 Corbis:** Science Faction/Dan McCoy. **66 Dreamstime.com:** (bl). **66-67 iStockphoto.com:** Luis Carlos Torres (c/Balls). **67 Corbis:** Science Faction/National Nuclear Security Administration (br) (bl/Barium) (clb/Calcium). **68 Alamy Images:** Phil Degginger (cl/Lithium). **Dorling Kindersley:** The British Museum, London/Chas Howson (cra/Nickel). **Getty Images:** amanaimages (bl/Swing). **68-69 Getty Images:** photo division (tc/Playground). **iStockphoto.com:** Ermin Gutenberger (Asphalt). **69 Dorling Kindersley:** Courtesy of the Natural History Museum, London/Colin Keates (cr/Carbon). **Getty Images:** Blend Images/Ross Anania (tl/Playground). **iStockphoto.com:** (tc/Balloon); Bruce Lonngren (tc/Light Bulb); Caleb Sheridan (tr/Neon). **Science Photo Library:** Charles D. Winters (cla/Chromium). **70 Getty Images:** OJO Images/Simon Murrell (cl). **iStockphoto.com:** AlexStar (cb). **70-71 iStockphoto.com:** Ingvald Kaldhussæter (Background). **71 Corbis:** Daniel J. Cox (r/Aurora Borealis). **Getty Images:** Stone+/Chip Forelli (bc/Ice Cube). **iStockphoto.com:** (r/TV); David Crockett (bl/Toast); Павел Игнатов (bl/Plate). **72 Dorling Kindersley:** Courtesy of Oxford University Museum of Natural History/Gary Ombler (clb/Corundum). **Getty Images:** Stockbyte/Martin Poole (cl/Tongs); Stone/Will Crocker (cl). **iStockphoto.com:** (cla/Flask); Vlad Konstantinov (cl/Flask); Kenneth C. Zirkel (cra/Foam). **73 Corbis:** In Pictures/Richard Baker (tr/Pylon). **Getty Images:** Image Source (bl/Beaker); Stockbyte/Martin Poole (tl/Tongs). **iStockphoto.com:** (br). **74 iStockphoto.com:** Maria Petrova (bl). **74-75 iStockphoto.com:** Rob Freiberger (bc/Bin); Dragan Trifunovic (Background). **75 Corbis:** Roger Ressmeyer (cb/Biodegradable Fork). **Getty Images:** The Image Bank/David Leahy (b). **iStockphoto.com:** Frank van den Bergh (cb/Rusted Sign); Karl-Friedrich Hohl (cl/Bunsen Flame). **76 Dorling Kindersley:** Courtesy of the Natural History Museum, London/Harry Taylor (bl/Beaker). **iStockphoto.com:** (bl/Bottles); Carmen Martínez Banús (bc/Book Pile); Greg Cooksey (c/Book); Mark Evans (r/Drip); Kashtalian Liudmyla (br/Airplane). **76-77 Getty Images:** The Image Bank/Cosmo Condina (Background). **iStockphoto.com:** pixhook (b/Background Wood). **77 Dorling Kindersley:** Courtesy of Dr Brian Widdop of the Medical Toxicology Unit Laboratory, New Cross Hospital/Gary Ombler (cl). **Getty Images:** WIN-Initiative (br/Salt). **78 Dorling Kindersley:** The American Museum of Natural History/Denis Finnin and Jackie Beckett (bc/Beaker Label). **iStockphoto.com:** Jeremy Voisey (bl/Beaker Label). **78-79 Dorling Kindersley:** Courtesy of the Science Museum, London/Clive Streeter (c/Litmus). **iStockphoto.com:** Robert Kacpura (b/Wooden Surface). **79 Dorling Kindersley:** Courtesy of the Natural History Museum, London/Colin Keates (cb/Mercury Sulphide); Courtesy of the Science Museum, London/Clive Streeter (cr/Copper Sulphate). **iStockphoto.com:** Jolanta Dabrowska (bl/Car Battery); winterling (bl/Batteries). **80 Corbis:** First Light/Peter Carroll (cl/Glass); Lester Lefkowitz (c/Oil Refinery). **Getty Images:** Photographer's Choice/Steven Puetzer (bc/Asphalt); Miguel Villagran (cl/Fuel). **iStockphoto.com:** blackred (bc/Glass); Natallia Bokach (cr); Norman Chan (crb); Andrea Krause (c/Glass). **80-81 iStockphoto.com:** Juan Facundo Mora Soria (b/Background). **81 Alamy Images:** Jim West (t/Glass Blower); Wildscape (bc/Recycled Tyre). **Getty Images:** Digital Vision/Nicholas Eveleigh (bc/Medical Stint). **iStockphoto.com:** blackred (cr/Glass); Andrea Krause (bc/Glass); Martin McCarthy (c). **US Department of Energy:** Atmospheric Radiation Measurement Program (cr/Proteus). **82-83 Corbis:** Lester Lefkowitz. **84 Corbis:** Transtock/Frank Hoppen (tc/T-Shirt Image); Visuals Unlimited (tr/T-Shirt Image). **iStockphoto.com:** Lukasz Panek (tl/T-Shirt Image). **84-85 Getty Images:** Photographer's Choice/Ty Allison (Background Runners). **85 Getty Images:** (tl/T-Shirt Image); Randy Faris (cl/T-Shirt Image). **iStockphoto.com:** Marcus Clackson (tl/T-Shirt Image). **SOHO (ESA & NASA) :** (c/T-Shirt Image). **86 Dreamstime.com:** Jlye (tr/Moon). **NASA:** (tr/Earth). **86-87 Getty Images:** Photographer's Choice/Matthias Tunger (Background). **87 Dorling Kindersley:** Ted Taylor - modelmaker/Tim Ridley (tr). **Getty Images:** CSA Images (cl). **iStockphoto.com:** pavlen (tl/Parachute); James Trice (c). **88 Corbis:** Transtock (c/Background Exterior Car). **Getty Images:** AFP/Adrian Dennis (bc). **88-89 Getty Images:** Stone/Jon Feingersh (Background Car Interior). **89 Corbis:** Gerolf Kalt (tr); Joe McBride (bl). **iStockphoto.com:** Joachim Wendler (cb). **90 Getty Images:** Image Source (cr/Rocks). **iStockphoto.com:** Don Bayley (bc); PeskyMonkey (cl). **90-91 iStockphoto.com:** Andy Medina (Background). **91 Getty Images:** Blend Images/Rick Gomez (cla). **iStockphoto.com:** (tr); Roman Milert (cl). **92 Corbis:** Reuters/Alessandro Bianchi (br/X-Rays). **Getty Images:** David McNew (bl/Gamma Rays). **92-93 Getty Images:** The Image Bank/Jorg Greuel (Background). **93 Getty Images:** Image Source (cl/Infrared Rays); Stock Image/Franz Aberham (cr/Visible Light). **iStockphoto.com:** Michael Blackburn (br/Microwaves); Pawel Kaminski (tl/Ultraviolet); Stephen Kirschenmann (bl/Radiowaves). **94 Getty Images:** Photographer's Choice/Franco Banfi (tl/Whale). **iStockphoto.com:** (c/Guitar). **NASA:** (tc/Shuttle). **94-95 Getty Images:** Caspar Benson (Music Awards); Digital Vision (Drum Kit). **95 Getty Images:** Ivan Grlic (tr); Christopher O'Driscoll (crb/Speaker); Urs Siedentop (tl/Acoustic Foam). **Photolibrary:** Mauritius/Chris Hermann (br). **96 Getty Images:** amanaimages/Mitsushi Okada (tr/Jar). **96 Getty Images:** Photographer's Choice/Images Etc Ltd (ca/Hot Air Balloons). **iStockphoto.com:** Ryan Kelly (b/Thermometer). **96-97 Getty Images:** Johner Images (Mountaineer). **97 Corbis:** WildCountry (tc/Gliders). **98 iStockphoto.com:** (br/Glasses).

98-99 Dreamstime.com: Nopow (Crowd). **iStockphoto.com:** Robert Kohlhuber (Lasers). **99 iStockphoto.com:** (tr); Max Delson Martins Santos (tl). **100 Getty Images:** AFP/Jens Schlueter (bl); Tim Graham Photo Library (cr). **iStockphoto.com:** Dino Ablakovic (tr). **100-101 iStockphoto.com:** (Background Brick Wall). **101 Alamy Images:** Niels Poulsen (tl). **iStockphoto.com:** Rowan Butler (Metal Plates); Anthony Douanne (cra); Stasys Eidiejus (cr/Hazard Sign); Erik de Graaf (clb); Kevin Green (tc/Green Paint); Christophe Testi (tr); Arkadiy Yarmolenko (bl). **102 Science Photo Library:** Jeremy Walker. **103 Corbis:** Werner H. Müller (c/Magnetic Field). **Dorling Kindersley:** Courtesy of the Science Museum, London/Clive Streeter (bl). **iStockphoto.com:** Yury Kosourov (cr); Alex Max (c/Metal Plate). **104 Corbis:** Mike Grandmaison (tr); Ultimate Chase/Mike Theiss (cl). **Getty Images:** Nick Veasey (cb). **iStockphoto.com:** (crb/TV) (cl/TV); Luis M. Molina (tr/TV). **104-105 Getty Images:** The Image Bank/Tom Bonaventure (Reflection). **iStockphoto.com:** Don Bayley (Shelving); Michal Rozanski (b/Pavement). **105 Alamy Images:** Lyroky (tl). **Corbis:** Reuters/Stefan Wermuth (br). **Dorling Kindersley:** Courtesy of the Science Museum, London/Clive Streeter (b). **Getty Images:** Photodisc/Christopher Robbins (cr). **106-107 NASA:** ESA, M. Robberto (Space Telescope Science Institute/ESA) and the Hubble Space Telescope Orion Treasury Project Team; ESA, ESO, F. Courbin (Ecole Polytechnique Federale de Lausanne, Switzerland) and P. Magain (Universite de Liege, Belgium) (bc). **108 NASA:** ESA, F. Paresce (INAF-IASF, Bologna, Italy) , R. O'Connell (University of Virginia, Charlottesville) and the Wide Field Camera 3 Science Oversight Committee (c); The Hubble Heritage Team (clb). **108-109 iStockphoto.com:** Jon Helgason (Emulsions). **109 NASA:** ESA, and the Hubble Heritage Team (STScI/AURA) -ESA/Hubble Collaboration (br). **109 NASA:** ESA, and The Hubble Heritage Team (STScI/AURA) (tr); Designed by Carl Sagan and Frank Drake. Artwork prepared by Linda Salzman Sagan. Photograph by NASA Ames Resarch Center (NASA-ARC) (c). **110 Corbis:** Aflo Relax/Komei Motohashi (clb); Atlantide Phototravel (tr/Taxi); Visuals Unlimited (bc). **110-111 iStockphoto.com:** Doug Cannell (Granite). **111 Corbis:** Science Faction/Tony Hallas (cra); ESA, and The Hubble Heritage Team (STScI/AURA) (cl); ESA, and the Hubble SM4 ERO Team (crb); ESA, C. Heymans (University of British Columbia, Vancouver) , M. Gray (University of Nottingham, U.K.) , M. Barden (Innsbruck) , the STAGES collaboration, C. Wolf (Oxford University, U.K.) , K. Meisenheimer (Max-Planck Institute for Astronomy, Heidelberg) , and the COMBO-17 collaboration (c); ESA, The Hubble Heritage Team, (STScI/AURA) and A. Riess (STScI) (bl). **NASA:** ESA, A. Aloisi (STScI/ESA) , and The Hubble Heritage (STScI/AURA) -ESA/Hubble Collaboration (tr). **112 Corbis:** Image Source (Game Pieces). **iStockphoto.com:** Jon Helgason (bl). **NASA:** ESA, F. Paresce (INAF-IASF, Bologna, Italy) , R. O'Connell (University of Virginia, Charlottesville) , and the Wide Field Camera 3 Science Oversight Committee (c). **Science Photo Library:** John Chumack (tr). **112-113 iStockphoto.com:** Doga Yusuf Dokdok (Carpet). **113 iStockphoto.com:** Milos Luzanin (bl). **114 Courtesy of Apple. Apple and the Apple logo are trademarks of Apple Computer Inc., registered in the US and other countries:** (cl/iPhone). **NASA:** JPL (cl/Asteroid). **114-115 iStockphoto.com:** Janne Ahvo (c/Book). **115 iStockphoto.com:** Özgür Donmaz (tr). **NASA:** ESA, and A. Schaller (for STScI) (ca/On Screen); JPL (cl) (c). **116 Dorling Kindersley:** Peter Griffiths - modelmaker/Clive Streeter (cr). **SOHO (ESA & NASA) :** (cb) (bc) (crb). **116-117 Getty Images:** Photonica/Anna Peisl (c/People). **iStockphoto.com:** Sze Kit Poon (b/Sand). **117 Alamy Images:** Laszlo Podor (bc). **Corbis:** Science Faction/William Radcliffe (c). **NASA:** JPL (clb). **118 Corbis:** Index Stock/Victoria Johana (bc); Science Faction/Tony Hallas (cl). **Getty Images:** Photographer's Choice/Roger Ressmeyer (cr). **NASA:** JPL/JHUAPL (cla). **118-119 Corbis:** Beateworks/William Geddes (Background). **119 Dorling Kindersley:** Courtesy of the Natural History Museum, London/Colin Keates (c). **Photolibrary/Jim Wark** (tr). **NASA:** ESA, and Marc W. Buie (Southwest Research Institute) (cl). **120 Getty Images:** Panoramic Images (cb) (bl/Blueprint). **iStockphoto.com:** Nicholas Belton (tr/Blueprint); Gustaf Brundin (bl/Calipers); Michal Rozanski (cb/Tablet PC). **121 Chandra X-Ray Observatory:** X-ray (NASA/CXC/MIT/D.Dewey et al. & NASA/CXC/SAO/J. DePasquale); Optical (NASA/STScI) (tr). **Corbis:** Roger Ressmeyer (cra) (bc/Coffee Cup). **iStockphoto.com:** (tl/Pen) (clb); Jamie Farrant (c/Notebook); Nicolas Hansen (tc/Glasses); Valerie Loiseleux (tr/Template). **NASA:** Hubble (bc); JPL-Caltech (crb); USRA (cl). **122 Getty Images:** Photographer's Choice/Erik Simonsen (cr). **NASA:** JAXA (c); Johnson Space Center (br); Kennedy Space Center (tl). **122-123 Dreamstime.com:** (Background). **123 NASA:** Dryden Flight Research Center (cr); JHUAPL/SwRI (tr); JPL (br)

All other images © Dorling Kindersley
For further information see: www.dkimages.com

For further information see:

www.dkimages.com